The Obamacare Disaster

An Appraisal of
the Patient Protection and
Affordable Care Act

Peter Ferrara

Heartland Policy Study #128
The Heartland Institute

The Obamacare Disaster

Published by The Heartland Institute
19 South LaSalle Street #903
Chicago, Illinois 60603
phone 312/377-4000
fax 312/377-5000
www.heartland.org

Opinions expressed are solely those of the author. Nothing in this report should be construed as necessarily reflecting the view of The Heartland Institute or as an attempt to influence pending legislation.

Additional copies of this report are available from The Heartland Institute for the following prices:

1-10 copies	$5.95 per copy
11-50 copies	$4.95 per copy
51-100 copies	$3.95 per copy
101 or more	$2.95 per copy

Printed in the United States of America

Contents

Introduction

"We have to pass the bill so that you can find out what is in it," House Speaker Nancy Pelosi said at a meeting of the National Association of Counties on March 9, 2010.[1] Now that the Patient Protection and Affordable Care Act (henceforth "the Act" or "Obamacare") is law, "what is in it" is revealed by 3,256 pages of legislative text, counting the 858 pages of the reconciliation bill (as printed at my local library).

This study is a comprehensive review of the Act and an early appraisal of its likely effects. It is the second report by the author on Obamacare, the first being a critique of bills still being debated by Congress in August 2009.[2] Most of the bill's provisions, except its tax increases, do not go into effect until 2014. So what follows is like a visit from the ghost of Christmas Future, shadows of what will be, but do not have to be, if we will change it. Obamacare instead could be repealed and replaced with far superior reforms … which in fact are the author's recommendations.

A summary of principal findings follows this introduction. Part 1 reviews the provisions of Obamacare and how they expand government's authority over health care providers and consumers. Part 2 explains how Obamacare will lead to higher health insurance premiums and health care costs. Part 3 explains the comprehensive system of government health care rationing created by Obamacare, including how the Act eviscerates incentives for investment and innovation in health care.

Part 4 describes the new taxes and higher tax rates imposed by Obamacare. Part 5 explains how Obamacare will cause runaway government spending and sharply increase the deficit, contrary to the promises and rhetoric used to pass it. Part 6 explains how Obamacare will break many of the central promises made by Obama and leading Democrats used to pass it, including the promise that if you like your current health insurance you can keep it, and the promise that if you like your doctor you can keep him.

Part 7 describes the alternative health care reforms that could and should be adopted if Obamacare were repealed and replaced. The theme of these alternatives is to expand and maximize the power and control over health care choices by patients and the doctors they have chosen. Those reforms also include a comprehensive health care safety net that would ensure access to essential health care for everyone. A brief summary and conclusion ends the report.

Executive Summary

This appraisal arrives at ten principal findings:

1. Government Takeover of Health Care. Obamacare authorizes an astonishing expansion of government authority over doctors, hospitals, insurers, employers, and individuals. It creates more than 150 new bureaucracies, agencies, boards, commissions, and programs to rule over health care in America. Government authorities are empowered to tell doctors and hospitals what is quality health care and what is not, what are best practices in medicine, how their medical practices should be structured, and what they will be paid and when. Government authorities will mandate exactly what health insurance with what benefits workers and employers must buy, and the Act imposes tax penalties on them if they do not comply. Government authorities will dictate to insurance companies exactly what health insurance they must sell, to whom they must sell it, and what they can charge. Obamacare even redistributes premium income among insurers under a new "risk adjustment" mechanism. This adds up to nothing short of a government takeover of health care.

2. Soaring Health Care Costs. Despite Obamacare's promise of making health care more affordable, the increased regulations, "free" benefits, and guaranteed coverage for various groups will cause health insurance rates to rise sharply, simply so insurers will have the funds to pay promised benefits. Demand for health care services will rise due to the incentives from third-party payment for health care by insurers and the government, while the supply is reduced by constraining the payment for services and through other disincentives. That is a prescription for soaring health care costs.

3. Government Health Care Rationing. Obamacare attempts to anticipate and prevent rising health care costs by giving government the authority to ration care. This begins by constraining the resources going to doctors and hospitals through nearly $3 trillion in Medicare cuts over the first 20 years. A new, democratically unaccountable Independent Medicare Advisory Board is created with authority to adopt still more Medicare cuts. Payment practices adopted by Medicare will be copied by private insurers, spreading the impact throughout the entire health care system. The Act creates financial incentives for doctors and hospitals to deny health care, contrary to the interests of their patients. Government authorities will use their new power over payments to doctors and hospitals to favor those who follow their rationing dictates.

These constrained resources will decimate incentives for investment in health care facilities such as hospitals and clinics, and in the provision of current technologies and services. Already we have seen the cancellation of 60 proposed new doctor-owned hospitals across the country because of new burdens imposed by the legislation. This means less access for Americans to advanced medical technologies such as MRIs and CT scans.

4. Short-circuiting Innovation. Obamacare also will discourage private investment in the development of new medical technologies and drugs. Politicians will use limited resources to keep popular services free or nearly free and copayments low, diverting funds from research and development where social benefits are longer-term and more difficult to see. As investment in health care technology declines, Americans will lose access to new innovations that modern medical science could support, such as gene therapies and biotechnologies.

All of this rationing will get worse over time, as rising costs force government to constrain the resources to health care even further. We see this already in Massachusetts, which adopted the essentials of Obamacare in 2006.

5. Higher Taxes. Obamacare imposes new taxes and increases tax rates starting in 2011, adding up to $500 billion over the first ten years. Some of these tax increases will add further to rising higher health insurance premiums and higher health costs as they are passed through to patients. Even with the new entitlement subsidies in the Act, buying the required high-cost insurance will be like a new payroll tax on working people, from

2.8 percent at lower incomes up to almost 10 percent on everyone making more than 200 percent of poverty (about $44,000 for a family of four). The penalty for not complying with the individual mandate is $695 per person in a family, up to a maximum of $2,085 a year. That applies to everyone regardless of income. These new taxes violate candidate Barack Obama's pledge in 2008 not to raise taxes on anyone making less than $250,000 per year.

6. Runaway Government Spending. Even though we cannot remotely afford all of the entitlement promises we already have made through Social Security, Medicare, and Medicaid, Obamacare sharply expands Medicaid and in addition creates a massive new health insurance entitlement subsidy program. The Congressional Budget Office (CBO) reports the Act will increase federal spending by almost $1 trillion over the first ten years. Over the first ten years of full implementation, starting the clock in 2014, the Act involves $2.4 trillion in increased spending, making the Act the most expensive legislation ever approved by Congress and signed by a president. As all the effects of the legislation play out, actual spending will be much higher.

7. Higher Deficits. President Obama barnstormed the country insisting Obamacare would actually reduce federal deficits, based on a CBO score. But he did not tell us the CBO score assumed $2.9 trillion in Medicare cuts over the first 20 years, which is highly unlikely to occur and, if it did, would create chaos in health care for seniors. More realistic forecasts show Obamacare would add between $2 trillion and $3 trillion, perhaps more, to the national debt over the next 20 years. It is not exaggerating to say Obamacare could bankrupt the nation.

8. Lower Quality Care. The American people currently enjoy the most technologically advanced and highest quality health care in the world. Many Americans are alive today only because of this high-quality health care. This is a central component of the traditional high standard of living in America. Obamacare will sharply reduce the quality of care particularly for the most vulnerable, such as premature babies and the elderly, and those suffering from cancer or heart disease. The authors of the Act promised "health care for all," but in fact the new system will institutionalize a rationing system that will deny health care to the sickest and those who need it most.

9. Slashing Jobs, Wages, and Economic Growth. While President Obama repeatedly claimed Obamacare was essential to restoring long-term economic growth, the Act will have the opposite effect, slashing jobs, wages, and long-term growth. That will be the effect of the employer mandate and the increased taxes under the Act on investment income. The Small Business Tax Credit highly touted by President Obama also will produce these effects, as the full credit is available only for very small firms paying very low wages, and the credit phases out as the number of workers or average wages increase. That effectively imposes a penalty on creating new jobs or paying higher wages, discouraging both. Similarly, the health insurance subsidies under the Act also phase out as income rises, effectively doubling marginal tax rates in the income tax code for low, moderate, and middle-income workers.

10. Broken Promises. Candidate Obama promised not to raise taxes in any form for anyone making less than $250,000 per year, and to not sign the legislation if it would increase the deficit by a single dime. Signing Obamacare clearly broke those promises. Candidate and then President Obama promised that if you like your current health insurance, you can keep it. But under the terms of the Act, many employers will drop their current coverage due to the financial incentives created by the Act. Some insurers will terminate current lines of insurance or go out of business altogether.

The Chief Actuary of Medicare admits that once the Act is phased in, at least half of seniors with Medicare Advantage will lose that coverage. Members of Congress and their staffers will lose their current generous coverage under the Federal Employee Health Benefits program.

President Obama promised repeatedly that if you like your current doctor you could keep him or her. But will your doctor keep you under Obamacare? Many doctors are likely to terminate their Medicare practices under the Act, or at least refuse to see new Medicare patients. Many specialists you have come to know and expect to rely on will no longer be available to serve you because of payment practices under the Act. Because of reduced payments and loss of freedom to control their own practices, many doctors will retire early or leave their practices for other professional opportunities.

Tragically, none of this was necessary. Coverage could have been extended to all of the uninsured who could not afford it simply by providing some assistance for them to buy it, with a tax credit or voucher. Many policy analysts, including this author, have been advocating this and other "patient power" reforms for many years.[3] This would have required relatively small additional costs largely offset by savings. But President Obama and Congressional Democrats refused to consider this type of reform, which does not involve expanded government power and control over health care.

Part 1

A Government Takeover of Health Care

A complete summary of the provisions contained in the Patient Protection and Affordable Care Act would require a series of encyclopedia-sized books. In this section, we will outline the basic structure, with the crippling details to follow.

Obamacare creates 159 new bureaucracies, boards, agencies, commissions, and programs to govern American health care.[4] Included among them are the Health Choices Administration, Health Benefits Advisory Committee, Independent Medicare Advisory Board, Bureau of Health Information, National Priorities for Performance Improvement office, Interagency Working Group on Health Care Quality, Institute of Medicine, Community Preventative Services Task Force, Physician Quality Reporting Initiative, Center for Quality Improvement, National Health Care Workforce Commission, Patient-Centered Outcomes Research Institute, National Center for Health Workforce Analysis, and state-based reinsurance programs. This does not include the Federal Coordinating Council on Comparative Effectiveness, which was created by the stimulus bill.

These government authorities will tell doctors and hospitals what are the "best practices" in health care, what "works" in health care and what doesn't, what health care is "comparatively effective" or "cost effective," and what is and is not "quality health care."[5] Doctors, specialists, surgeons, and hospitals also will be told how their medical practices should be structured, and what they will be paid and when.

Obamacare imposes costly new regulatory burdens on insurers that working people, not insurance companies, will pay for through higher premiums. Most prominently, these include "guaranteed issue,"[6] which means all insurers must offer coverage to everyone who applies no matter how sick they are or how costly they may be to cover. That includes coverage for all pre-existing conditions for all applicants.[7] The regulatory burdens also include "community rating,"[8] which means insurers cannot vary their rates based on the medical condition or illnesses of applicants. They can vary rates within a limited range only for age, geographic location, and family size. The regulatory burdens also include "free" preventive care[9] and elimination of all lifetime limits and caps on health insurance benefits.[10] All of this costs money. How much it will increase health insurance costs is discussed in detail in Part 2 below.

Obamacare gives government the power to dictate to insurance companies what benefits and coverage they must provide,[11] who they must cover,[12] what they can charge,[13] and what deductibles, co-pays, and other out-of-pocket expenses their plans can include.[14] The government even redistributes premium income among insurance companies through "reinsurance" and "risk adjustment."[15] This is government taking over and running health insurance, contrary to President Obama's repeated statements to the contrary. While a social safety net is necessary to provide for those in need, it is better provided through means other than a government takeover of health insurance, as discussed in Part 7 below.

To try to force people to buy health insurance despite the higher costs due to these regulatory burdens, Obamacare gives government the power to require that people buy health insurance with the specific benefits the government decides you must have, whether you want those benefits or not.[16] You may think you don't need coverage for substance abuse treatment or mental health counseling, but the government now makes those choices for you under the Act, forcing you to pay for these costly benefits.[17] Single men with no children and women well past child-bearing age will pay for maternity benefits and well-baby and well-child care.

Millions of people today choose high-deductible health insurance plans in exchange for lower premiums, while self-insuring for small and routine medical expenses. Under Obamacare, these plans might still be offered, but few people will buy them since they won't be offered by the government-run insurance exchanges and their buyers won't qualify for subsidies.[18] If you don't buy the kind of insurance government wants you to buy, you will be ineligible for the subsidies your tax dollars are being used to provide to other people, *and* you may be subject to special tax penalties.

Obamacare requires employers to provide health insurance with the specific, costly, politically correct benefits the government decides they must provide.[19] Employers who have had success in controlling costs with particular plan designs will have to give them up, now that it is up to the government to decide what insurance they can provide. And if they don't provide the health insurance the government dictates, they will be subject to special tax penalties as well.

President Obama and House Speaker Nancy Pelosi keep repeating the mantra that Obamacare will provide "choice and competition." But with the government telling you what health insurance you have to buy, there will be little choice and less competition. Obama and Pelosi could have promoted choice and competition by allowing interstate sales of health insurance, but this apparently didn't advance their true objective of expanding the power and reach of government.

Recognizing this mandated health insurance will be expensive, Obamacare provides for extensive subsidies for the purchase of health insurance for families making up to four times the poverty level.[20] This means such welfare will be going to families of four making up to $88,000 today, increasing to $100,000 a year or more by 2018. Obamacare also expands Medicaid sharply to everyone up to 133 percent of poverty, including for the first time to childless adults who are capable of supporting themselves.[21] While this will add 24 million new dependents to Medicaid by 2015, Obamacare will still fail to achieve universal coverage, with the government itself estimating more than 23 million will still be uninsured by 2019.[22]

Obamacare provides for health insurance "exchanges" to be established in each state, a place where individuals could compare offerings by competing health insurers similar to the service provided already by healthinsurance.org on the Internet.[23] But the Act specifies in great detail exactly what insurers must offer on the exchanges, including benefit plans in four categories designated as Bronze, Silver, Gold, and Platinum.[24] The new entitlement subsidies discussed above are available only for insurance purchased on the exchanges, a policy that seems designed to put private insurance brokers out of business.

From telling doctors how to practice to determining how health insurance must be priced, and from mandating that everyone buy insurance to stacking the subsidy deck in favor of government-run insurance exchanges, Obamacare leaves virtually no aspect of health care beyond government control. It is no exaggeration to call this a government takeover of health care. Any elements of private choice and competition that are left by Obamacare are intended to disappear over time as new regulatory agencies expand their activities, as doctors conform to the new rules and incentives, and as consumers switch from private insurance to government-designed, subsidized, and marketed plans.

Obamacare does not create a single-payer health care system, a fact some leftists still lament. But it is something quite similar, basically a government-run health care system in everything but name. As the rest of this report documents, it's a system likely to produce high costs and little or no benefits.

Part 2

Increasing Health Costs

President Obama promised while campaigning for his health reform legislation that it would reduce the "growth of health care costs for our families, our businesses, and our government."[25] While he was campaigning for president, Obama and his allies in Congress promised repeatedly that their health plan would reduce the cost of health insurance by $2,500 per family.[26] But the Patient Protection and Affordable Care Act will have just the opposite effect, sharply increasing health costs for families, businesses, and government.

The federal government's own Centers for Medicare & Medicaid Services estimates Obamacare will cause health costs overall to rise by $311 billion over the next ten years.[27] But that study just scratched the surface. There are at least eight reasons why the Act will increase health care costs.

1. Expanded Medicaid Eligibility

Obamacare increases health care costs for the federal government by expanding coverage under Medicaid, the government program providing medical assistance to the poor, to those earning up to 138 percent of poverty.[28] Medicaid was already projected to cost almost $5 trillion over the next ten years, reaching $674 billion in 2017.

The Centers for Medicare & Medicaid Services estimates the bill will increase Medicaid enrollment by 24 million new beneficiaries by 2015, adding an additional $410 billion in further federal costs for the program over the next decade alone.[29] State governments will end up bearing some additional costs for this expansion, but the federal government will pick up most of these costs.

2. Subsidies for Middle- and Upper-Income Families

Obamacare increases costs for the federal government further by adopting a massive new health insurance entitlement program for families earning up to four times the poverty level. In 2014, this new program will be providing $3,000 in taxpayer funds to families making $95,000.[30] By 2018, almost $5,000 will be going to families making $102,000.[31]

CBO estimates these subsidies will cost taxpayers an additional $457 billion over the first six years alone.[32] The chief actuary of Medicare estimates the total cost of this new entitlement will reach more than $500 billion over the first six years, through 2019.[33] This is only the beginning, as this program will ultimately cost far more than now projected.

This is a massive increase in welfare extended to middle- and upper-income families, irresponsibly added on top of the runaway, financially intractable entitlement promises we already have made.

3. Supply and Demand Pressure

Obamacare will increase the demand for health care by covering the low-income uninsured through expanded Medicaid, subsidizing middle- and upper-income families, requiring that employers and individuals purchase insurance, and enriching the benefits provided by the insurance made available through the new insurance exchanges. With everyone covered or potentially covered by comprehensive mandated insurance, the perverse incentives of third-party payment to increase demand will increase.

When the government or an insurance company is paying most or all health care bills, individuals have an incentive to consume more health care until the net benefit from the last medical service consumed is equal to what the individual pays, which could be zero. In other words, people will demand and use health care services up to the point where it actually starts to cause harm, rather than balancing the possible benefit against the cost.

While the Act increases demand for health care, it also restricts the supply, as we will explain in Part 3. Rising demand combined with declining supply can have only one result: rising prices. These increased prices for health care mean health insurance costs will go up for families and businesses.

4. New Coverage Mandates

The health insurance Obamacare forces individuals to buy and employers to provide will contain mandated benefits that drive up costs and utilization.[34] On July 15, the Obama administration announced treatments for the prevention of alcohol abuse, depression, and obesity are among the services that will be "free" to consumers with new insurance plans starting in September.[35] All lifetime limits and caps on health insurance benefits would be eliminated as well.[36]

State mandates for expensive and infrequently used services such as drug rehabilitation and mental health services account for as much as a quarter of the cost of private health insurance today.[37] Coalitions of service providers and patients constantly lobby federal and state elected officials to add treatments to the list of services for which insurers must pay. Many of these services are not currently covered because their efficacy is uncertain, they are extremely expensive relative to the benefits provided, or they are too easily abused. Obamacare opens the door to these demands.

While the Obama administration insists these new benefits will be "free" for consumers, this is classic smoke and mirrors. Insurers must raise their premiums to pay for these new and expensive services. People buying the new insurance will see the services covered "for free" in their insurance policies, but their insurance premiums will be higher. Everyone's insurance premiums will go up to finance these new mandates.

5. Guaranteed Issue and Community Rating

Obamacare requires all insurers to cover all pre-existing conditions and offer coverage to everyone who applies, no matter how sick they are or how costly they may be to cover.[38] This regulatory requirement is known as "guaranteed issue." The Act also prohibits insurers from varying their rates based on the medical condition or illnesses of applicants. They can vary rates only within a limited range for age, geographic location, and family size.[39] This regulatory requirement is known as modified community rating.

These provisions are widely misunderstood. Under current law, an insurer cannot discontinue a policy or charge higher premiums simply because the insured becomes sick. Providing protection from the possibility of costly medical care is what health insurance is all about. Health insurers can no more be allowed to terminate or charge prohibitive fee increases to those who become sick while insured than fire insurers can be allowed to terminate or impose draconian fee increases on an insured once his or her house catches fire. That would not be insurance at all.

Insurers can, however, cancel coverage if it is discovered that the person with insurance lied about his or her medical condition or history during the application process. Cancelling policies in such situations, called "recission," is only fair.

Most of the much-publicized cases of people with serious health conditions being unable to buy insurance are of a different sort. They arise when people who weren't insured are diagnosed with an illness, and only then try to buy insurance. This is like waiting for your house to catch fire and then trying to buy home insurance. No surprise, no private insurers will step forward to offer to sell insurance in either case.

The legitimate but narrow concern of what to do with people who were uninsured at the time they were diagnosed with a serious illness, or who have let their insurance lapse, does not justify guaranteed issue or community rating. The former enables people who are young and healthy to game the system, waiting until they are sick before buying insurance. When they return to health, they can drop the insurance again. This drives up insurance premiums sharply because only the sicker will tend to be covered by insurance at any point in time, which means rates per insured have to be higher to cover costs.

Guaranteed issue and community rating regulatory requirements have been proven to raise insurance premiums sharply at in every state they have been tried.[40] The most egregious example is New York, where policies in the individual market for a single person in 2009 averaged $6,630 a year and $13,296 a year for family coverage, more than twice the national averages of $2,985 and $6,328, respectively.[41] The price difference was not due to differences in the underlying cost of care: Insurance prices in nearby Connecticut and Pennsylvania, which don't have guaranteed issue and community rating, were much closer to the national average.

Obamacare's proponents believe they have "solved" this problem by requiring everyone to be insured at all times. This "everybody in" strategy supposedly means nobody can free-ride off the system. But in fact, the penalties in the Act are *several times too small* to compel everyone to buy insurance, a point we return to in Part 5. There is no way to solve the free-rider problem, and this fact dooms guaranteed issue and community rating to failure.

The price-raising effects of the guaranteed issue and community rating requirements of Obamacare were documented a few months before its adoption by the accounting firm PriceWaterhouseCoopers, which examined the cost and accounting data of major health insurance firms. The study found the Act would increase the cost of a family health insurance policy costing $12,300 today to $17,200 by 2013, $21,300 by 2016, and $25,900 by 2019.[42] Can you imagine paying $25,900 a year for health insurance? Start planning, because this is what Obamacare is likely to cost nine years from now.

Another study conducted by Wellpoint, utilizing its own cost and claims data, found health insurance premiums for the young and healthy would triple in some states. Average middle-income families would see their premiums more than double.[43] For example, the premium for a healthy 25- year-old in Ohio would increase from $52 per month to $157, a 199 percent increase. A 40-year-old husband and wife with two kids would suffer a premium increase from $332 per month to $737, a 122 percent jump. A small business with eight employees in Franklin County, Ohio would suffer an 86 percent premium increase.

An earlier study in 2009 by the Council for Affordable Health Insurance similarly concluded the regulatory requirements of Obamacare would cause premiums in the individual market to nearly double.[44]

Confirmation that guaranteed issue and community rating will cause health insurance costs to rise is found in the experience of Massachusetts, which in 2006 adopted guaranteed issue and community rating, individual and employer mandates enforced by a penalty of more than $1,000 a year per resident, expanded Medicaid, extensive subsidies for the non-poor to purchase health insurance, and an exchange called a Connector.[45]

Health insurance for a family of four in Massachusetts today costs nearly $17,000, 33 percent more than the national average,[46] with premiums increasing at nearly double the national average since the reform.[47] The state's costs for health programs soared by 42 percent in less than three years under the reform,[48] one-third more than projected when the reforms were adopted.[49] And that is with the federal government heavily subsidizing the reform with $21.2 billion in the first three years, $3,000 per Massachusetts resident.[50]

Employers induced to support the Massachusetts reforms with the promise of lower health insurance costs have seen those costs increase by $500 million, with further increases expected.[51] In the first two years under the reform, premiums for employer-provided insurance grew 21 percent to 46 percent faster than the national average.[52] Despite claims the reforms would reduce health insurance costs in the individual market by 25 percent to 40 percent,[53] the same claims made by President Obama in the 2008 presidential campaign, the opposite has been true.

Just over half of the previously uninsured in Massachusetts say their health costs have gone up under the reform, with just 14 percent saying their costs have gone down.[54] Just 22 percent of the previously uninsured say the law has helped them, with 60 percent saying it has hurt them.[55] Since the reform was passed, per-capita health spending in the state has increased by 23 percent.[56]

Harvard-Pilgrim, one of the top insurers in Massachusetts, reported that between April 2008 and March 2009, about 40 percent of its new enrollees dropped their coverage in less than five months but incurred about $2,400 in monthly medical expenses, about 600 percent higher than normal.[57] This indicates many in the state are waiting until they need expensive medical care to buy insurance, then dropping it after the insurer pays the costs, knowing they can always get coverage later when they need further expensive care. Grace-Marie Turner writes, "There is growing evidence that many people are gaming the system by purchasing health insurance when they need surgery or other expensive medical care, then dropping it a few months later."[58]

6. Taxes on Health Insurance

Obamacare imposes a dozen new taxes described in greater detail in Part 4. Here we limit our discussion to taxes on health insurance that will raise the cost of the very thing they are supposed to be making more affordable.

The so-called "Cadillac tax" is projected to raise $32 billion in new tax revenues over the first ten years.[59] The tax is set at 40 percent of the cost of insurance above $10,200 for individuals and $27,500 for families.[60] Those thresholds are indexed to grow with general inflation, not health costs, after 2020, so over time more and more health plans will be subject to the tax, ultimately including standard, average, health plans. The higher health insurance costs resulting from this tax will come out of the wages otherwise paid to workers.

Obamacare also imposes a second, additional tax on the health insurance premiums paid to all insurers, calculated by dividing the total tax to be collected among insurers based on the proportion of total health insurance premiums collected by each.[61] This tax will increase health insurance costs by $60 billion over the first ten years.[62] These increased costs will again be paid by working people, either directly in higher costs for health insurance, or in the form of reduced wages to make up for the additional costs incurred by their employers.

7. Taxes on Drugs and Medical Devices

Obamacare imposes a $27 billion a year tax on manufacturers and importers of pharmaceutical drugs, divided among them based on market share.[63] Like the taxes on insurance, this tax will increase the cost of health care, requiring higher health insurance premiums and raising overall health costs.

Similarly, Obamacare imposes a new 2.3 percent tax on medical device manufacturers,[64] raising health costs an additional $26.3 billion a year.[65] There are more than 80,000 medical devices manufactured in the United States, including artificial heart valves, pacemakers, incubators, and thermometers.[66] The additional cost will be borne by the sick and passed through to all consumers via higher health insurance premiums.

8. Increased Cost-Shifting

Obamacare expands Medicaid eventually to 24 million additional people, and that will mean additional cost-shifting to privately insured persons and the uninsured.

Because Medicaid and Medicare already badly underpay doctors and hospitals, providers must increase the prices charged to privately insured persons and the uninsured to make up the losses. A projected (but unlikely) $2.9 trillion savings in federal Medicare reimbursements (see Part 6 for an explanation) will come mostly from lower payments to doctors and hospitals, which would compel them to further raise prices for the uninsured and those with private insurance.

A study conducted by one of the nation's top actuarial firms, Milliman, Inc., concluded that cost-shifting to private insurance due to the low compensation paid to doctors and hospitals by Medicaid and Medicare raised the cost of private health insurance by $88.5 billion per year, or $1,788 for an average family of four.[67] That was *before* passage of Obamacare. Adding 24 million new dependents to Medicaid and cutting Medicare reimbursements by $2.9 trillion will cause cost-shifting to soar.

9. Conclusion

The combined impact of all these spending increases is uncertain, but the numbers we are reasonably sure of are enormous. Expanding Medicaid enrollment will cost $41 billion a year, subsidies to middle- and upper-income families will add $83 billion more, and new taxes on drugs and medical devices, $53.3 billion more.

Big as they are, these spending increases are small compared to the price increases caused by mandating guaranteed issue and community rating, which research we've cited indicates will double the cost of health insurance for many people with individual coverage. The impact of mandating expensive and easily abused kinds of coverage, and cost-shifting by Medicaid and Medicare, could easily lead to rate increases of similar magnitudes.

Just days after Obamacare was signed by President Obama, major American employers began modifying their financial statements as required by law to document the losses they would already start incurring under just one provision of the Act, raising taxes on their retiree health benefits. Among the businesses reporting expected losses were AT&T, $1 billion;

Verizon, $970 million; Deere & Co., $150 million; Boeing, $150 million; Caterpillar, $100 million; Lockheed Martin, $96 million; Illinois Tool Works, $22 million; Honeywell, $13 million; and Goodrich, $10 million.[68] The cost increases had already begun, exactly contrary to President Obama's promises.

As CBO Budget Chief Douglas Elmendorf testified before Congress in the summer of 2009 regarding the then-pending legislation: "In the legislation that has been reported we do not see the sort of fundamental changes that would be necessary to reduce the trajectory of federal health spending by a significant amount. On the contrary, the legislation significantly expands the federal responsibility for health care costs."[69]

Part 3
Government Rationing of Health Care

In apparent anticipation of the exploding health costs that will result from the government's takeover of health care, the Patient Protection and Affordable Care Act provides for a comprehensive system of government rationing of health care. That rationing starts with huge Medicare cuts that begin to starve the system of the resources needed to maintain current levels of care. It extends to compensation policies that reward the insurers and physicians who avoid caring for the unhealthy and elderly. And it ends with the kind of comprehensive rationing that has caused the quality of care in Canada and Europe to decline relative to the United States.

1. Medicare Cuts

CBO scored Obamacare as including $500 billion in Medicare cuts in the first ten years, but this includes the first years before any cuts are made. Over the first ten years of full implementation, the cuts actually total $800 billion. Over the first 20 years of implementation, the total climbs to an astounding $2.9 trillion.[70]

Such Medicare cuts would create havoc and chaos in health care for seniors. Hospitals, physicians, surgeons, and specialists providing critical care to the elderly such as surgery for hip and knee replacements, sophisticated diagnostics through MRIs and CT scans, and treatment for cancer and heart disease will close their doors entirely or stop serving Medicare patients.[71]

If the government is not going to pay, then seniors are not going to get the health services, treatment and care they expect. The Mayo Clinic, for example, has announced its Arizona facilities will no longer see Medicare beneficiaries because reimbursement rates are too low. According to a

Mayo spokesperson, the clinic lost $840 million in 2008 treating Medicare patients.[72]

Amazingly, Obamacare contains a provision that could lead to even bigger cuts to Medicare. It creates an Independent Medicare Advisory Board, an appointed (not elected) body with the power to adopt further Medicare cuts it deems necessary. These cuts would become effective without further Congressional action. The report of the chief actuary of Medicare from the Centers for Medicare & Medicaid Services states, "The Secretary of HHS is required to implement the Board's recommendations unless the statutory process is overridden by new legislation."[73]

Even before passage of Obamacare, the Obama administration started rationing health care for seniors on Medicare.[74] According to *The Wall Street Journal,* the new Medicare payment rules for this year impose an 11 percent overall cut on cardiology and a 19 percent cut on radiation oncology (cancer treatment). Payments for basic tools and treatments for heart disease, such as stress tests and cardiac catheterization, would be slashed by 42 percent and 24 percent respectively. Payments for diagnostic imaging services like MRIs and CT scans that help identify cancer early would be cut by 24 percent. Payments for anti-tumor radiation therapy will be cut by 44 percent.

2. Incentives to Ration Care

Several provisions of Obamacare give insurers, doctors, and hospitals incentives to deny health care to their patients, contrary to the patients' interests. Starting with insurers, new regulatory requirements under the Act greatly disfavor new insurance competitors by limiting what can be spent on marketing and administration for such things as monitoring costs and stopping fraud. Selling a new insurance product requires higher marketing costs to penetrate the market. With the Act's new restrictions on such costs, few new competitors are likely to try. Indeed, because all health insurance must conform to the Act's specifications regarding benefits, deductibles, and co-pays, there is less scope for new insurers to compete with new products serving different consumer preferences.

John Goodman, president of the National Center for Policy Analysis, and Gerald Musgrave have described the incentives for insurers created by guaranteed issue and community rating, where insurers cannot refuse coverage or charge more for applicants who are sick with costly illnesses.[75] Insurers will affiliate with preferred provider networks not well-equipped to provide essential care for the sickest and most costly, and they will seek reputations for serving well the young and healthy instead. Goodman and

Musgrave explain, "The easiest way [for insurers] to keep costs down is to enroll only the healthy. And the easiest way to do that is not to have the doctors and facilities sick people want." Similarly, health economist Alain Enthoven writes, "A good way to avoid enrolling diabetics is to have no endocrinologists on staff. ... A good way to avoid cancer patients is to have a poor oncology department."[76] While network access standards defined by statute or regulations may prevent insurers from going this far, it is clear that networks will be narrowed to attract or repel some classes of patients to drive better economics, reducing patient choice.

Mandates require insurers to cover expensive primary-care services and other benefits, yet insurers face political pressure, including the threat of overt legal restrictions as we already see in Massachusetts and California, to avoid premium increases. To meet these cost pressures, insurers are reorganizing to gain greater power to do so. Scott Gottlieb, a former official at the federal government's Centers for Medicare & Medicaid Services, reports insurers "are trying to buy up medical clinics and doctor practices. Where they can't own providers outright, they'll maintain smaller networks of physicians that they will contract with so they can manage doctors more closely."[77]

HMOs, which have more control over the medical facilities with which they are affiliated, are likely to benefit from the new rules. They will feature facilities and programs that appeal to the young and healthy, such as gyms, dancing lessons, sports contests, etc., and avoid facilities best-suited for treating patients with cancer or heart disease. They know they stand to gain the most if they get reputations as not serving those sickest patients well, so those patients go elsewhere. Because HMOs have the most power to control their costs in this way, we may find other insurers phasing out over time, leaving patients with less real choice and power regarding their health care.

Obamacare tries to counter these effects through mechanisms such as risk adjustment and reinsurance that would redistribute resources among insurers to those with the sickest and most-costly patients.[78] These provisions show even the authors of the Act recognize these incentive effects are a real problem. But as Goodman and Musgrave explain,

> The problem with this approach is that it does not work very well. Health economist Joseph Newhouse notes that in the RAND Health Insurance Experiment, 1 percent of the patients accounted for 28 percent of the total costs, but most of the high cost patients could not have been identified in advance, even when researchers had full knowledge of the patients' demographic characteristics. More recently, Newhouse and his colleagues have concluded that as much as 25 percent of the variation in health expenditures for

> individuals can be predicted by such observable factors as health status and prior health expenditure. That leaves 75 percent unexplained.[79]

So risk adjustment can't ensure adequate payment up front for the risks of a sicker population. And if we just compensate insurers and HMOs after the fact for the costs they actually incur, we have a system of cost-plus financing with strong incentives for runaway costs. Moreover, experience with both Medicaid and Medicare shows the government cannot be relied upon to compensate for costs after the fact.

Not satisfied with the big increase in power Obamacare gives to HMOs, the Act's architects add provisions to encourage the "medical home" model, a sort of high-powered HMO model of health care financing that combines insurers with medical providers, giving them the power and incentives to ration health care. Medical homes begin under the Act as demonstration projects, but HHS is authorized to "disseminate this approach rapidly on a national basis."[80] The Act further provides that patients in a medical home may have to settle for a nurse practitioner rather than a physician as the primary care provider.[81]

Doctors face pressure to ration care due to slashed payments and other cost pressures imposed by insurers, HMOs, and the provisions of Obamacare. The Senate version of the bill that preceded passage of the Act included a provision in Section 3003 penalizing doctors who spend the most in Medicare funds on their patients.[82] That would have created a new competition among doctors to see who could provide the least to their patients. While that provision was deleted from the final Act, Section 3003 still sets up an elaborate system to calculate and report to doctors and hospitals how much in Medicare expenses can be attributed to each doctor. That already begins pressure to reduce spending by denying and rationing care and sets up the system to which penalties on individual doctors can be added later.

Doctors are responding to all these new pressures by selling their solo or small group practices to networks or becoming salaried employees of hospitals or clinics. The trend was already underway before Obamacare was enacted: More than two-thirds of medical practices were physician-owned in 2005, while fewer than half were in 2008.[83] Gottlieb observes how Obamacare has turned that trend into a stampede toward the exits:

> By next year [2011], more than 60 percent of physicians will be salaried employees. ... Last month, a hospital I'm affiliated with outside of Manhattan sent a note to physicians announcing a new subsidiary it's forming to buy up local medical practices. Nearby

> physicians are lining up to sell – and not just primary care doctors, but highly paid specialists like orthopedic surgeons and neurologists. Similar developments are unfolding nationwide. ... Like the insurers, physicians are responding to the economic burdens of the president's plan in one of the few ways they're permitted to.[84]

The effect of this transition on patients may be mixed, but it is mostly bad. Gottlieb says "consolidated practices and salaried doctors will leave fewer options for patients and longer waiting times for routine appointments."[85] Salaried doctors are unlikely to be willing to be on call 24 hours a day, to develop long-term relationships that can lead to greater familiarity with patients' conditions, and to be advocates for their patients against insurers and hospital administrators who place a higher emphasis on limiting spending than relieving pain or finding a cure. As the medical profession transitions toward salaried positions, it's unlikely to pay enough to attract individuals of exceptional talent and dedication, who will go to other professions.

Dr. Gordon Hughes, chairman of the board of trustees for the Indiana State Medical Association, told *The New York Times*, "When I was young, you didn't blink an eye at being on call all the time, going to the hospital, being up all night. But the young people coming out of training now don't want to do much call and don't want the risk of buying into a practice, but they still want a good lifestyle and a big salary. You can't have it both ways."[86]

The result of all this consolidation will be a small number of insurers, hospital chains, and clinic chains with much greater power to implement rationing, and government policies favoring more such rationing than is currently possible. Consumers will be left with little choice or power. As Merrill Mathews explains, "Although Democrats claimed their reform would bring competition to the health care system, in fact the system will rapidly move to a bevy of oligopolies where a handful of large players will survive, and maybe even thrive. The losers will be competition, innovation, and ... patients."[87]

3. Comparative Effectiveness and Rationing

Under Obamacare, the Federal Coordinating Council for Comparative Effectiveness is empowered to tell doctors and hospitals what are the "best practices" in medicine, "what works in health care and what doesn't," and what treatment, practice, or care is comparatively more effective than another.[88] A centralized government bureaucracy will make such determinations on the basis of trials and observational data.

As Newt Gingrich observes, Obamacare "has put comparative effectiveness research in the United States on the same path as in Britain: toward becoming a bureaucratic cost control measure. The United Kingdom, which has a nationalized, single-payer health system, explicitly uses comparative effectiveness to ration medical care. Government uses this research to decide, sometimes with devastating consequences, which treatments its citizens can get."[89]

Comparative effectiveness means analyzing which alternative health care treatment is comparatively more effective than another. This is what doctors do all the time, and it is central to the practice of medicine. But when a government bureaucracy that doesn't know you or your medical condition tries to take over this function, it is a counterproductive perversion of medical care that empowers the government to ration and deny your health care.

Comparative effectiveness research (CER) will always be behind the curve of the latest scientific advances, knowledge, and practice. Careful, independent, controlled studies are expensive and time-consuming. By the time they are completed, the science and the data have raced on. As Dr. Leonard A. Zwelling, professor of medicine and pharmacology at the University of Texas M.D. Anderson Cancer Center, has written recently, "But while carefully controlled, independently monitored clinical trials are the gold standard of CER, they are very expensive, time consuming and do not guarantee that the one best therapy will be identified. In the case of prostate cancer progress is so rapid that the use of historical data for definitive answers is not a worthy expenditure of time or money."[90] Professor Zwelling adds,

> Since CER uses analyses of older, previously completed studies or collections of clinical data from disparate hospital records, CER is unlikely to help the individual with a newly diagnosed cancer in 2010. That patient may choose among therapeutic options that were unavailable even a few years ago.[91]

Even more troubling is that the concept of comparative effectiveness can be stretched to include the question of what is comparatively more effective given the cost of the care. We saw the beginnings of this type of health care rationing last year when the U.S. Preventative Services Task Force abruptly reversed its long-standing recommendations that women over 40 get mammograms to test for breast cancer every year. Now it recommends no more mammograms for women under 50 or over 74, and only every other year for the ages in between. Under the prior practice, breast cancer death rates fell by 30 percent over the past 20 years.[92] Dara Richardson Heron recounted in the *New York Post* how her breast cancer was discovered, and her life saved, by a mammogram at age 34.[93] But the government panel indicated it takes 42 percent more mammogram tests to save a life for women in their 40s compared to those in their 50s, so saving those lives before 50 is apparently not worth the costs of the tests any more. The task force's recommendation of no mammograms for women over 74 says if you have breast cancer at that age, the bureaucrats in charge of access to health care services don't even want to know about it.

Under Obamacare, this same task force is empowered to determine your coverage for preventive services. How else does the Act allow bureaucrats to use comparative effectiveness research to ration care? Betsy McCaughey points out that under the Act health insurers can pay only doctors who follow the regulations the secretary of HHS imposes under Section 1313 of the Act to improve health care "quality."[94] "Quality" is a very broad term that can cover everything in medicine. Regulations under this authority can provide that new innovations and technologies do not yet qualify as "quality" medicine, effectively delaying their implementation to control costs. "Quality" also can be defined as not involving care the government deems "wasteful," or not sufficiently effective, or not yet warranted, contrary to what your doctor says. Care also may be deemed not "quality" if it doesn't follow the conclusions of the Federal Coordinating Council for Comparative Effectiveness Research regarding what health care is comparatively more effective in treating particular illnesses and conditions.

Numerous provisions in Obamacare grant the newly created bureaucracies broad powers to control "quality," which takes power and control over health care away from patients and the doctors and hospitals they choose for their care. Under the rubric of "quality," the government can effectively delay, ration, or deny care to reduce costs or otherwise suit government policy preferences. The decisions of all these bureaucracies can be enforced through the payment system by using concepts such as "pay for performance" and "accountable care."

An often-overlooked report issued in June 2009 by the President's Council of Economic Advisors foreshadowed the use of these methods to hold down costs.[95] That report claimed 30 percent of American health care is "waste" that can be identified and eliminated by wise, centralized, government bureaucracies. The now-enacted legislation creates bureaucracies with the power to do precisely this.

This movement toward "one size fits all" medicine is made necessary when a government agency operating under budgetary constraints must decide what health care services to cover and not to cover. But a bureaucracy cannot know better than your own doctors what will work best for you, an individual patient. Making such judgments for your particular case is exactly what you hire your doctors to do. Indeed, the most advanced practices are trending towards "personalized medicine" involving increasingly possible gene therapies based on your personal genetic makeup, and such advances as "molecular analysis" of the particular cancer a patient may suffer.[96]

4. Incentives to Invest and Innovate

The fourth way Obamacare leads to rationing is by discouraging investment and innovation. Investors are not going to finance acquisition of the latest, most advanced equipment and technologies if the government slashes compensation for the services such technologies provide or if insurers take pains to avoid having to pay for them. Investors won't finance new or expanded hospital facilities or clinics, or even the full maintenance of existing ones. This is how the long waiting lines for diagnostics, surgery, and other referrals begin to develop in countries with socialized health care. It is why hospitals and other medical facilities in those countries are often old and deteriorating.

We are already starting to see some of these results. Because of the incentive effects and costly new regulatory burdens of the new legislation, plans for 60 new doctor-owned hospitals across the country already have been scuttled.[97] Obamacare also slashes compensation under Medicare for MRI and CT scan facilities in doctors' offices. Such facilities ease burdens on patients, who don't have to struggle to get appointments and sit in waiting rooms elsewhere, and improve health by accelerating diagnosis.[98] But with the compensation to doctors for such services slashed, patients will increasingly lose this convenient and superior health care.

Low reimbursement levels and the bias of the new bureaucracies against new drugs and therapies will destroy incentives for investors to put their money into research and development to discover the next generation of advanced, high-tech medical care. Vast new opportunities for innovative health services and care opened up by modern science, such as gene therapies and biotechnology, will go unrealized. Drug companies will cut back on investment in cutting-edge, curative, pain-relieving, and life-saving miracle drugs.

Some major drug companies already have announced plans to invest in marketing existing drugs in other countries rather than bring new drugs to market in the United States.[99] Just when the rapid advancement of science and technology is opening up new vistas to counter disease, suffering, and death, self-congratulatory politicians and bureaucrats are closing them. Many people will suffer or die unnecessarily as a result.

Obamacare gives HMOs and insurers' preferred provider networks strong incentives to be slow in adopting such technologies, innovations, and breakthroughs for the sickest and most costly, since doing so risks developing a reputation for being the place for the sickest and most costly patients to go. Investment instead will go toward things that attract younger and healthier patients: gyms, sports medicine, athletic equipment, coffee shops, and more comfortable waiting rooms.

Investment in human capital also would be negatively affected. Underpaid doctors, surgeons, and specialists would choose less-demanding and perhaps more-remunerative fields. Some would see fewer patients, devote more time to their families, and take more vacations. Others would simply retire earlier than planned. Survey evidence reveals that, thanks to underpayment from Medicaid and Medicare, this is already starting to happen.[100] With less investment in technology and facilities and lower pay in the future, some of the bright young students who would have pursued careers in medicine and health care will choose other professions instead.

A smaller supply of health professionals would exacerbate the problems of longer lines, waiting times, and less health care. Combined with the effects of greater demand for health care from millions of people wanting their "free" health care and from the formerly uninsured, the severity of inadequate supply of health care would become even more acute.

These incentive effects indicate a reduced supply of health care overall, which (as described in Part 2) means even further increases in prices and costs. Colliding with the increased demand for health care described above, the result is what Milton Friedman called "the black hole of socialized medicine," with everyone paying more and more for less and less.[101]

5. Rationing in Massachusetts

Massachusetts offers a preview of the rationing Obamacare is likely to bring forth. The 2006 government takeover of health care in that state involved policies very similar to those contained in Obamacare, and in fact parts of the latter were modeled after the Massachusetts programs.

A wave of increased demand for medical services from the newly insured and others with more generous third-party payment in Massachusetts is swamping the state's supply of doctors, which has been stagnant at best. In 2008, the Massachusetts Medical Society reported nearly half of all internists in the state were not accepting new patients, with waiting times for an appointment increasing sharply to 52 days.[102] By the fall of 2008, the *Boston Globe* was reporting the wait to see a primary care doctor had grown to as long as 100 days.[103] "As a result," John Goodman writes, "the waiting times to see a new doctor in Boston are twice as long as in any other U.S. city."[104]

Grace-Marie Turner reports the complaint of one Massachusetts resident, "Before I was uninsured and couldn't see a doctor. Then I made the sacrifice to buy insurance, but I still can't find a doctor who will see me. So I still don't get to see a doctor, but it's costing me more now."[105]

Dr. Sandra Schneider, vice-president of the American College of Emergency Physicians, explains the futility of the Massachusetts program: "Just because you have insurance doesn't mean there is a [primary care] physician who can see you."[106] Turner summarized the problem, "As one would expect, expanded insurance has caused an increase in demand for medical services. But there hasn't been a corresponding increase in the number of doctors. As a result, many patients are insured in name only. They have health coverage, but can't find a doctor."[107] Greg Scandlen adds, "Due to the sudden increase in demand for physicians, every resident who would like to see a doctor is being harmed."[108]

Because they can't get in to see a doctor, "Thousands of newly insured Massachusetts residents are relying on emergency rooms for routine medical care, an expensive habit that drives up health care costs and thwarts a major goal of the state's first in the nation health insurance law," the *Boston Globe* reported in April 2009.[109] John Goodman reports, "there are still as many people going to emergency rooms for care in Massachusetts today as there were before the Massachusetts health plan was adopted."[110] In fact, *The Boston Globe* reports there are more.[111] Michael Bond of the National Center for Policy Analysis reports, "Long delays [to see a doctor] are causing people to rely on the emergency room (ER) for nonemergency care. More than half of the patients visiting a Massachusetts ER in the last two years could have been treated in a doctor's office."[112]

Obtaining routine care in emergency rooms is more costly than at a doctor's office. Advocates of the Massachusetts government health care takeover argued it would eliminate or at least minimize use of hospital emergency rooms by the formerly uninsured, and reduce health costs and health insurance premiums for everyone as a result. But the opposite has happened, and the cost of caring for emergency room patients increased by nearly 18 percent over the first two years.[113]

The problem will be even bigger under Obamacare in other states. Scandlen explains,

> Massachusetts has by far the largest number of physicians per capita of any state. By contrast, California has half as many

> physicians per capita and twice the level of uninsured. Imagine what will happen to waiting times in California if all the uninsured suddenly become insured. ... Waiting times in ERs will soar. Other big states like Texas and Florida are even less able than California to serve the newly insured. What kind of health reform requires working people to pay for coverage, but then deprives them of the ability to see a doctor?[114]

The Massachusetts health reform continues in a downward spiral, threatening more overt rationing. Soaring health costs (discussed in Part 2) caused insurers to file for double-digit rate increases in Spring 2010. But state regulators, backed by Gov. Deval Patrick, refused any rate increase, even though one senior state official warned of "catastrophic consequences" for the state's insurers. The remaining four major insurers in the state are losing $150 million a month and soon will not have the money to pay all promised benefits.[115]

Regarding the requested rate increases, Massachusetts Insurance Commissioner Jack Murphy said, "I don't know how much clearer we could have been with them. We communicated four times what rates we expected."[116] Indeed, state regulators stated they will impose fines "and potentially other penalties" on the insurers for having the temerity to ask for enough in premiums to pay the promised benefits.[117] Sally Pipes explains the irrationality that prevails in the state's politics now: "When insurers then complained that they'd post losses, the Patrick administration blasted them as 'outrageous,' 'uninterested in alleviating escalating health-care costs,' and 'in love with the status quo.'"[118]

The state's regulators and policymakers are looking to the insurers to cut their payments to doctors and hospitals to make up for the losses.[119] But the doctors and hospitals are already suffering financially under the health reform. Expanded Medicaid and even the state-subsidized plans in the Commonwealth Care Connector, the analogue to the Obama exchanges, already pay less than the actual cost of care. As Pipes explains, "When you lose money on every unit, you can't make it up on volume."[120]

When the doctors and hospitals are not paid enough to cover their costs, they will provide less care, which is another form of rationing. One answer already introduced in the state Senate: force doctors and hospitals to accept Medicaid patients as a condition to keeping their medical licenses. As Pipes comments, "When voluntary exchange doesn't work for politicians, they move to conscription."[121] It is almost unbelievable that such a proposal is being made in America.

Progressives in Massachusetts are now threatening to use the crisis as a bridge to outright socialized medicine. Pipes reports, "Massachusetts state Senate President Therese Murray has proposed putting an end to 'fee for service' medicine in the next five years and moving to a system of capitated managed care, where doctors receive a flat fee for each assigned patient."[122] That limits costs, for sure, but also the amount of health care that is delivered, because when the money runs out, the doctor simply says, "I am sorry but there is nothing more we can do." That would be official health care policy for the state under a mandatory "global budget" that is also under discussion among reformers and political leaders.[123] That would effectively turn the state into a government-run HMO,[124] indistinguishable from a single-payer system.

6. Rationing in Other Countries

The descent into rationing and socialism we are witnessing in Massachusetts has occurred in every country that has adopted a government takeover of health care. Nadeem Esmail, director of health system performance studies at the Fraser Institute in Canada, provides an example from the Canadian system:

> In Ontario, Lindsay McCreith was suffering from headaches and seizures yet faced a four and a half month wait for an MRI scan. ... [H]e went south, and paid for an MRI scan across the border in Buffalo [New York]. The MRI revealed a malignant brain tumor. Ontario's government system still refused to provide timely treatment, offering instead a months-long wait for surgery. In the end, McCreith returned to Buffalo and paid for surgery that may have saved his life.[125]

Esmail offers another example,

> In March of 2005, [Ontario resident Shona] Holmes began losing her vision and experienced headaches, anxiety attacks, extreme fatigue, and weight gain. Despite an MRI scan showing a brain tumor, Ms. Holmes was told she would have to wait months to see a specialist. In June, her vision deteriorating rapidly, Ms. Holmes went to the Mayo Clinic in Arizona, where she found that immediate surgery was required to prevent permanent vision loss and potentially death. Again, the government system in Ontario required more appointments and more tests, along with more wait times. Ms. Holmes returned to the Mayo Clinic and paid for her

surgery.[126]

And another example,

> "[Alberta resident] Bill Murray waited in pain for more than a year to see a specialist for his arthritic hip. The specialist recommended a 'Birmingham' hip resurfacing surgery [a state-of-the-art procedure that gives better results than basic hip replacement]. But government bureaucrats determined that Mr. Murray, who was 57, was 'too old' to enjoy the benefits of this procedure and said no. In the end, he was also denied the opportunity to pay for the procedure himself. He's heading to court claiming a violation of constitutional rights.[127]

While Tom Daschle and Obama's Council of Economic Advisors tout European health care rationing as a model for the U.S., they fail to report the long queues and limited access to specialists and the latest medical equipment in those countries, which result in health outcomes that are inferior to those of the U.S. For example, one-quarter of those diagnosed with breast cancer in the U.S. die of it, while the comparable figure is 35 percent in France and 46 percent in Britain and New Zealand.[128] About 19 percent of American men die from prostate cancer once diagnosed. The figures are 30 percent and 35 percent in New Zealand and Australia, respectively, and 49 percent and 57 percent in France and Britain, respectively.[129]

In Canada, the median average wait for treatment after referral to a specialist was 18.3 weeks in 2007.[130] Patients in Saskatchewan waited the longest – 27.2 weeks – followed by New Brunswick (25.2 weeks) and Nova Scotia (24.8 weeks). Britain's National Health Service (NHS) has more than one million people on waiting lists for care. The cumulative waiting time expected by all Britons already in the queue for medical treatment exceeds one million years.[131]

The number of physicians per capita is nearly 50 percent higher in the U.S. than in Britain and Canada.[132] Moreover, of these available doctors, only 11 percent in the U.S. are general practitioners, while in Canada and Great Britain nearly half are, which means American patients have much greater access to specialists.[133] American patients also have much greater access to the latest medical technology. American patients receive 83.2 MRI exams per 1,000 people versus 25.5 for Canadian patients and 19.0 for British patients.[134] American patients also receive 172.5 CT scans per 1,000 people versus 87.3 for Canadian patients and 43.0 for British patients.[135]

These restrictions on access to medical care have real-world consequences for patients. The Council for Affordable Health Insurance reports,

> In Great Britain's National Health Service, breast cancer patients have been denied access to widely used cancer drugs, and lack of access to dentists has led patients to pulling out their own teeth. In Canada, 12 percent of the Ontario population can't get a family physician, and Nova Scotia resorted to a lottery so people could get a doctor's appointment.[136]

Despite these facts, President Obama's head of the Centers for Medicare & Medicaid Services, Dr. Donald Berwick, says, "I am a romantic about the NHS. All I need to do to rediscover the romance is to look at the health care of my own country," which he calls "crazy" and "immoral."[137] He is also romantic about the National Institute for Clinical Excellence (NICE), which is the bureaucracy in charge of rationing and denial of health care for the British people.[138] Berwick says, "NICE is extremely effective and a conscientious, valuable, and – importantly – knowledge-building system."[139] For America, he says, "The decision is not whether or not we will ration care – the decision is whether we will ration with our eyes open."[140] As Grace-Marie Turner writes, "We are in big trouble as Dr. Berwick will be in charge of administering big chunks of ObamaCare."[141]

The extensive rationing found in socialized health care systems around the world reflects the fundamental political calculus behind Obamacare. Greater control over health care spending decisions allows politicians to lavish spending on the healthy, who constitute the vast majority of voters at any point in time and who cost relatively little to serve adequately. Governments then inevitably seek to cut sharply spending for the sickest and most vulnerable, who are a very small proportion of the population at any one time. John Goodman explains, "Politicians cannot afford to spend most of the health care budget on the small number who need expensive care. Democratic politics forces them to take from the sick and give to the healthy instead."[142]

The politics of nationalized health care is cold but effective. Those suffering from cancer or heart disease and denied care by their government will likely never be able to trace the effect of such cuts on their care, or understand what has been lost. And even if they do somehow, they are too few and perhaps too weak to do anything about it.

7. Rationing by Government versus by Private Providers

Supporters of Obamacare argue that insurance companies and private health care providers already ration and deny care based on the ability to pay. Even conservatives have been too quick to accept the mantra that the current health care system rations access to care by price. The whole point of health insurance, however, is to avoid rationing by price in health care.

The great majority of non-elderly Americans are currently covered by private health insurance and there is virtually no rationing by price for them. Many of those without insurance can afford to purchase care as they need it, or can receive free care from various social safety-net systems. This system is not ideal, and many proposals have been advanced over the years to insert incentives to minimize wasteful use of services and encourage competition on price in health care markets. But the fact remains that the current system cannot be said to ration access to care by price.

Insurance companies in the present health care system have nowhere near the power to discriminate or withhold care that the government has been given by Obamacare. Under the traditional fee-for-service health insurance model, if your licensed doctor prescribes specific care or treatment, and the terms of your insurance policy cover it, the insurer has no power to deny the care or payment for it. It is not up to insurance companies to determine if a particular drug or service is worth the cost. "Rescissions" – where an insurer cancels a health policy after the patient becomes sick – are allowed only in cases where the insured falsified his or her health history on the insurance application.

If you choose an HMO or other insurance that requires service or treatment from a specified network of providers, then you have agreed to give up some control over your health care in return for lower costs. But even in such cases, if you don't like how your insurer handles that control and power, you can switch to another insurance company or pay for drugs or services yourself.

This system of choice and competition is very different from one where government controls a nation's health care system. Everyone may have health insurance in a government-controlled system, but *access* to health care is actually reduced due to less supply, long waiting periods, and less investment discovering or bringing to market new forms of health care. If you don't like the care you are receiving, you cannot choose a competing service provider: *There is no competition, hence no competitors eager for your business.*

"Choice" in a nationalized health care system means getting to vote for a different candidate every two or four years, hoping he or she wins, and hoping public policy will change as a result. Even then you are in a zero-sum game with other people hoping to get public funding shifted to their community, or to their particular disease and needs.

8. Conclusion

Liberal defenders of Obamacare pooh-pooh claims it will lead to government rationing of health care. They say claims of rationing are only a scare tactic used by conservatives to frighten senior citizens into voting Republican. But they are wrong. The facts could hardly be more clear.

Cutting nearly $3 trillion from Medicare spending during the next 20 years will necessarily require rationing the care given to seniors. There is simply no way around it, and liberal spokespersons ought to be called on to admit it. Similarly, by imposing guaranteed issue and community rating on insurers and other regulations and compensation cuts on hospitals and doctors, Obamacare will lead to reductions in care decided by an oligopoly of big insurers, big hospitals, and giant networks of clinics. How can that *not* be accurately called rationing?

If rationing is not at the heart of Obamacare, why does the legislation call for "comparative effectiveness" research and give bureaucracies the authority to restrict care on the basis of cost-benefit analysis? How can Obamacare not lead to rationing when the state program it is modeled after, the 2006 Massachusetts reforms, has led to exactly that outcome? And ditto every other country in the world that has allowed government to take over health care?

Rationing is ugly, cold-hearted, and unfair. It strikes at the very heart of what makes health care in America the best in the world. It violates the trust between doctors and their patients, without which treatment often fails. Rationing is what Obamacare is all about, and it is a major reason why Obamacare should be repealed or reformed.

Part 4
Higher Taxes

When he was asking for our votes in 2008, candidate Barack Obama famously promised the American people, "I can make a firm pledge. Under my plan no family making less than $250,000 a year will see any form of tax increase. Not your income tax, not your payroll tax, not your capital gains taxes, not any of your taxes."[143]

Candidate Obama didn't just make that pledge once or twice. He promised it to the American people over and over, making it the centerpiece of his campaign. Many voters thought Obama was more likely than John McCain to cut taxes or keep taxes low, an amazing achievement for a senator with the most liberal voting record of the U.S. Senate. The Patient Protection and Affordable Care Act violates Obama's pledge not just once, but many times.

1. The Individual Mandate

If you do not obtain the health insurance Obamacare requires, either through your employer or by direct purchase yourself, then beginning in 2014 you must pay a new tax. The tax starts at $95 or 1 percent of annual income, whichever is greater, increases to $325 or 2 percent of income in 2015, and then $695 or 2.5 percent of income after that. This applies to everyone, including those making less than $250,000 per year.[144]

The mandate to buy insurance is indistinguishable from a tax. Even with the budget-crushing new entitlement subsidies in the Act, the insurance will be quite expensive, ranging from 2 percent of income for people at 133 percent of poverty to 9.5 percent of income for people at 400 percent of poverty.[146] That is like a new payroll tax.

It's easy to pass a law that says everyone must buy health insurance; it is impossible to enforce such a law. The tax penalties for failing to buy insurance cannot be set high enough, at least for low- and middle-income earners who pay little or no personal income taxes, to make individuals less well off if they refuse to buy insurance. And penalties on employers who refuse to buy insurance for their employees would have to be so high that millions of small businesses would simply be bankrupted by such a law.

The Act states in Section 1501 that criminal penalties will not apply for failing to pay the fine, and it cannot be enforced by imposing liens on the taxpayer's property, so the penalties are not even enforceable. But such individuals can still buy insurance after they or a member of their family gets sick. The American Academy of Actuaries, in a letter to Nancy Pelosi and Harry Reid in January 2010, wrote:

> [T]he financial penalties associated with the bill's individual mandates are fairly weak compared to coverage costs. ... In particular, younger individuals in states that currently allow underwriting and wider premium variations by age could see much higher premiums than they face currently (and may have chosen to forego). The premiums for young and healthy individuals would likely be high compared to the penalty, especially in the early years, but even after fully phased in, thus likely leading many to forgo coverage.[147]

Anyone as smart as a fifth grader can see it is cheaper not to buy insurance and simply pay the fines. The cost of buying qualifying health insurance coverage for a family is likely to be well over $12,000 per year, several times the penalty. Workers and employers can save too much by just foregoing the coverage and paying the penalty, assuming they are caught and forced to pay it.

2. The Employer Mandate

The second Obamacare tax is paid by employers.[148] Starting in 2014, if an employer does not offer "qualified" health coverage, and at least one employee qualifies for a health tax credit, the employer must pay a non-deductible tax of $2,000 for every uninsured full-time employee over 30 employees. (A company with 100 employees would therefore pay $2,000 x 70 = $140,000 a year.) The CBO estimates the tax will raise $52 billion in the first six years.

The tax applies to all employers with 50 or more employees. If any employee actually receives coverage through the exchange, the penalty on the employer for that employee rises to $3,000. If the employer requires a waiting period of 30-60 days to enroll in coverage, there is a $400 tax per employee ($600 if the period is 60 days or longer).

"Qualified" health insurance is insurance coverage that complies with the new mandates imposed on insurers by the Act. Existing coverage is "grandfathered," and therefore presumably exempted from the new mandates, but employers lose this protection if they change insurance carriers or change the deductible or co-pay requirements under the existing plan. A report by HHS predicts two-thirds of businesses with current coverage will not qualify for the grandfather exemption.[149]

Even companies that offer qualified insurance to their employees will be subject to taxes and penalties if even one employee applies for tax credits by purchasing insurance from the government-run insurance exchanges. As many as one-third of employers are expected to pay fines under this provision.

The fact that employers pay these taxes, rather than employees, will not insulate employees from the cost. Nothing in Obamacare enables employers to find new money to pay for new insurance benefits. They will pay for them by attempting to pass along the cost to customers, by raising prices, by reducing wages, or by reducing dividends or other payments to investors and shareholders. We explain the impact on jobs and economic growth more fully in Part 5.

3. More Taxes

Candidate Obama first issued his no-tax-increase pledge in a speech attacking John McCain for proposing to tax so-called Cadillac health plans, employer-provided plans that are especially generous and costly. Obama said then, "The better your health care plan, the harder you fought for your good benefits, the higher the taxes you'll pay under John McCain's plan,"[150] an attack he repeated in several commercials.

But Obamacare raises taxes on precisely those health plans, regardless of the income of workers who have them, albeit not until after 2018. The tax is set at 40 percent of the cost of insurance above $10,200 for individuals and $27,500 for families and is projected to raise $32 billion in new tax revenues over the first ten years.[151]

Other taxes contained in Obamacare include three taxes reported and discussed in Part 2:

- A tax, paid by insurers, on health insurance premiums, expected to collect $60 billion over ten years.

- A tax on medical device manufacturers, expected to raise $26.3 billion a year.

- A tax on prescription drugs, expected to raise $27 billion a year.

These taxes actually are imposed on health care services or insurance, which means they will raise the cost of the very goods and services they are meant to subsidize. This is like taking money out of one pocket and putting it in another, or taxing Peter to pay Paul.

More new taxes include the following:[152]

- Starting immediately, a 10 percent tax on tanning salons, expected to raise $2.7 billion a year.

- Starting in 2011, funds in health savings accounts (HSAs), flexible spending accounts (FSAs), and health reimbursement arrangements (HRAs) can no longer be used to buy non-prescription, over-the-counter medicines except insulin, meaning those drugs must be purchased with taxable income. The tax penalty on non-medical early withdrawals from an HSA increases from 10 percent to 20 percent. Deposits into FSAs, currently unlimited, will be capped at $2,500 and indexed to inflation after 2013.

Starting in 2013, the following taxes take effect:[153]

- A 3.8 percent Medicare "payroll" tax surcharge will apply to investment income, expected to raise $123.4 billion over seven years.

- The Medicare Hospital Insurance payroll tax is increased by 31 percent on income over $200,000 for singles and $250,000 for couples, expected to raise $86.8 billion over seven years.

- The itemized deduction from federal income taxes for medical expenses is reduced by raising the threshold from 7.5 percent of adjusted gross income to 10 percent, a tax increase expected to raise $15.2 billion a year. (The hike is waived for taxpayers 65 years old or older from 2013-2016.)

- The tax deduction for employer-provided retirement prescription drug coverage, adopted as part of the new prescription drug benefit under Medicare Part D, is reduced, expecting to raise $4.5 billion a year.

- "Black liquor" tax hike, actually the repeal of a tax break the papermaking industry received under a 2005 transportation law meant to encourage the use of renewable resources. It is expected to raise $23.6 billion.

It is interesting to note that the revenues from applying the Medicare health insurance payroll tax to investment income will not go into the Medicare trust fund to finance Medicare. As the Medicare chief actuary states in his official report on behalf of the Centers for Medicare & Medicaid Services, "Despite the title of this tax, this provision is unrelated to Medicare; in particular, the revenues generated by the tax on unearned income are not allocated to the Medicare trust funds."[154]

But more importantly, these payroll tax increases will not raise nearly the $210 billion CBO projects.[155] Under President Obama's budget, the capital gains tax rate will be increasing by close to 60 percent, with the expiration of the Bush tax cuts and the Medicare payroll tax now applying to capital gains as well. But over the past 40 years, every time the capital gains tax rate has been increased, revenues have declined.[156]

Similarly, the tax rate on dividends next year will soar by nearly 200 percent, due again to the expiration of the Bush tax cuts and the application of the Medicare payroll tax to dividends as well. The last time dividend taxes were that high, corporations paid virtually no dividends. They just kept the money internally for corporate investment. Corporate earnings are already subject to a 35 percent corporate income tax rate. If the remaining 65 cents on the dollar is subject again to a 43.8 percent dividends tax rate, that would leave just 28.5 cents out of the original dollar earned. So revenues from the tax on dividends will decline sharply as well, the opposite of what happened when President George W. Bush cut the tax rate on dividends in 2003.

4. Conclusion

Candidate Obama promised no tax increases for families making less than $250,000 a year. The great majority of the taxes described above will be paid by middle- and even lower-income families. Hundreds of billions of dollars in new taxes will be collected to help finance a health care program that was supposed to *lower* the cost of health care!

The sheer range and magnitude of these tax increases almost defies imagination. At a time when the American people are extremely sensitive to proposals to raise taxes – large majorities of voters say they oppose any tax increase[157] – it is stunning that the biggest tax increase in the history of the country would have been passed with so few voters realizing it. It is unlikely that more than a few percent of the American people are aware of more than two or three of the 13 tax hikes listed here.

The last time a president so blatantly violated a no-tax-increase pledge was during the administration of President George H.W. Bush. After campaigning and winning in 1988 on a pledge of "Read my lips, no new taxes," he broke that pledge by agreeing to a budget deal in 1990. The public voted him out of office in the next election.

Part 5
Runaway Spending and Deficits

With large Democrat majorities in both houses of Congress, the Congressional Budget Office (CBO) is a Democrat-controlled institution. But even CBO admits Obamacare involves close to $1 trillion in increased federal spending.[158] That results primarily from the sharp increase in Medicaid enrollment and in the new entitlement subsidies for the purchase of health insurance, subsidizing families with incomes approaching $100,000 a year and more in the near future. But this is just the beginning of the likely costs.

1. Skyrocketing Spending

When Medicare was adopted in 1965, the official government estimates projected it would cost only $12 billion by 1990. The actual cost of the program that year was $109.7 billion, nine times greater than the original estimate.

Congressional rules require CBO to project costs over ten years for pending legislation. But the spending under Obamacare mostly does not get underway until 2014, so the official CBO score of just over $1 trillion includes only six years of full spending. Over the first ten years of actual implementation, 2014 to 2023, the Act calls for $2.4 trillion in increased spending.[159] From 2010 to 2029, a period that includes the first full 15 years of implementation, Obamacare will actually cost $5.3 trillion.[160]

But even these numbers don't take into account all of the effects of the legislation. Not included is any increased state spending for the expanded Medicaid program. Moreover, the health insurance subsidies go only to those who buy insurance on their own, individually, through the state-based exchanges set up by the legislation. Those who receive employer-provided coverage are not eligible for them. CBO assumes only 30 million workers will obtain their health insurance through the exchanges, with 162 million still receiving employer provided coverage.[161] Of those 30 million, CBO estimates 19 million would receive subsidies at a cost of $450 billion over the first ten years.[162] But with the mandated insurance likely to cost $15,000 or more by 2016,[163] employers will have powerful incentives to dump their employee coverage and pay the $2,000 per worker fine that applies to such termination of coverage.

Workers who lose their employer-provided insurance would be able to get the huge subsidies for purchasing their insurance through the exchange. As Douglas Holtz-Eakin explains,

> For example, a family earning about $59,000 a year in 2014 would receive a premium subsidy of about $7,200. A family making $71,000 would receive about $5,200; and even a family earning about $95,000 would receive a subsidy of almost $3,000. By 2018, ... a family earning about $64,000 would receive a subsidy of over $10,000, a family earning $77,000 would receive a subsidy of $7,800 and families earning $102,000 would receive a subsidy of almost $5,000.[164]

Holtz-Eakin calculates that employers could gain the enormous savings from dropping the coverage and just paying the $2,000 penalty, while giving their employees a net pay raise because of these enormous subsidies, for all workers making roughly $60,000 per year or less.[165] That means it would make sense for employers to drop their coverage for 43 million workers who would then receive the subsidies for obtaining their insurance through the exchange. That alone would result in roughly a trillion dollars in extra costs for Obamacare, immediately doubling the estimated costs of the Act.

The projected spending also does not take into account the effects of the increased demand through the counterproductive incentives of the third-party payment system, or of the reduced supply of health care, as discussed earlier, both of which will increase prices and consequently the cost of health care.

2. Soaring Deficits

President Obama promised the nation over and over that he would "not sign a plan that adds one dime to our deficits."[166] This pledge seemed to be fulfilled when CBO projected Obamacare would actually reduce the deficit by $143 billion in the first ten years, and by more than $1 trillion in the second ten years. But this was based on assumed Medicare cuts of almost $3 trillion over that period.[167] As discussed above, this would wreak havoc and cause chaos in health care for seniors. But if those cuts are reversed or not fully implemented, then the deficit would soar further.

Moreover, the deficit projection for the first ten years includes ten years of tax increases but only six years of spending increases. By the second ten years, the $2.372 trillion in Medicare cuts for that period becomes dominant.

There are other tricks in this deficit projection. It includes $29 billion in increased Social Security revenues, which under current law are devoted to financing Social Security, not any of Obamacare's new entitlements. Similarly, it includes $63 billion of increased Medicare payroll taxes on the wages of higher-income workers, which are actually devoted under the law to financing Medicare, not Obamacare's new spending.[168]

Moreover, yet another new entitlement created by Obamacare, for long-term nursing home care, known as the CLASS program, starts collecting premiums during those first ten years. Those $70 billion in revenues are counted as reducing the Act's deficit over those years, even though the funds are devoted to paying the longer-term benefits of that program.

The CBO deficit projections also do not include more than $100 billion in increased discretionary spending that will be necessary over the first ten years alone.[169] Yet the projections include $19 billion in supposed savings that would result from the government takeover of student loans, a provision completely unrelated to health care that was nevertheless included in the Act.

Even without reversing the Medicare cuts, correcting for these budget accounting gimmicks transforms the supposed $143 billion in deficit reduction in the first ten years to a nearly $100 billion addition to the deficit. Former CBO Director Douglas Holtz-Eakin estimates the actual result of Obamacare would be a deficit of $554 billion in the first ten years and $1.4 trillion in the second ten years.[170]

Reversing the Medicare cuts would mean deficits over the first ten years of at least $600 billion, and over the second ten years of $1.8 trillion, adding to the Holtz-Eakin estimate.[171] If more than 40 million more workers lose their employer insurance and gain the subsidies through the exchanges as discussed above, that would add another trillion to the deficit over the first full ten years alone.

Extreme budget dishonesty is reflected in the so-called "doc fix" controversy. President Obama and the Democrats rely on trillions in Medicare cuts, mostly involving slashed payments to doctors and hospitals for their medical services to seniors, to claim Obamacare does not increase the deficit, and actually reduces it. But now they seek to reverse some of those cuts in separate legislation that would add hundreds of billions to the deficit, called the "doc fix" bill because it would restore some of the compensation to doctors and hospitals for their services. Democrats say this doc fix bill is not part of the Act. But to rely on trillions in cuts to argue that Obamacare does not increase the deficit, and then to reverse some of those cuts in separate legislation, is an extremely dishonest budget shell game.

David Gratzer, writing for Forbes.com, comments accurately on how unlikely it is that Democrats will ever vote to cut Medicare spending:

> No Congress in recent years has been particularly effective about reining in Medicare costs. Congress reversed planned cuts in 1999. And 2004. And 2005. And 2006. And 2008. In fact, since 1997, when members of both parties agreed to automatic cuts if spending rose faster than population and economic growth, the program has been cut just once, in 2002.
>
> And this Democratic Congress has been no more disciplined. Senate Democrats just passed the "emergency" reversal to protect health care services in a recession. It's the same argument House Speaker Nancy Pelosi used to justify her own successful campaign to reverse fee cuts scheduled for December 2009. If Democrats didn't want to restrain health costs during a recession, why did they just spend a year writing a plan to do exactly that?[172]

Finally, the above analysis does not take into account the likelihood of lower revenues than projected as discussed in Part 4 or the likelihood of higher spending than expected as discussed in this section (except for the effects of the incentives for employers to drop employee coverage). Those effects, of course, would dramatically increase the deficit even further.

3. Mounting Debt

America can't finance all the long-term entitlement promises it already has made through Social Security, Medicare, and Medicaid. The Patient Protection and Affordable Care Act adds yet another impossible promise to the list, which can only be characterized as wildly irresponsible.

The latest Trustees' Reports show the unfunded liability for Medicare alone is $89 trillion.[173] Social Security adds another $15.1 trillion in unfunded liabilities, for a total of $104 trillion.[174] And that doesn't even count Medicaid. The entire American economy right now produces only about $14 trillion a year.

Going back 60 years, to World War II, total federal spending as a share of Gross Domestic Product (GDP) has been stable at about 20 percent. But the cost of the three big entitlement programs alone, Social Security, Medicare, and Medicaid, is now projected to eventually reach 20.5 percent of GDP.

Counting burgeoning interest on the national debt, on our current course federal spending will skyrocket towards 40 percent of GDP by 2040. Counting state and local spending, total government in America would consume more than 50 percent of GDP. GDP would collapse under the weight of all that spending and the resulting taxation and debt. With a crippled economy and confiscatory tax rates, America, quite simply, would no longer be a free country.

This doubling of federal spending as a share of GDP implies a doubling of federal tax rates. The Heritage Foundation reports trying to pay all of the promised benefits of Social Security, Medicare, and Medicaid by raising income taxes would require raising the top 35 percent tax bracket to 77 percent and the 25 percent tax bracket paid by middle-income earners to 55 percent.[175] All income tax brackets, in fact, would have to be doubled.

By 2018, less than ten years from now, Medicare Part A will be running a deficit of close to $100 billion. General revenue spending for Medicare Parts B and D that year are now projected to be $364 billion. Consequently, the deficit for Medicare alone that year will be close to $500 billion.

President Obama's runaway tax-and-spend economic policies are making all of this much worse. CBO now projects that under the latest Obama budget federal deficits over the next ten years would total almost $10 trillion ($9.761).[176] National debt held by the public would double in just four years, from $5.8 trillion at the end of 2008 to $11.6 trillion at the end of 2012. It would almost quadruple to $20.3 trillion by 2020, $1.7 trillion more than Obama projected in his budget in February.

In the process, the national debt would soar from 40 percent of GDP today to 90 percent by 2020, almost as big as our entire economy. But it gets even worse. Total Gross Federal Debt, which includes such items as the debt held in the Social Security trust funds (real debt that will have to be paid in the future), would be more than $27.5 trillion by 2020. That would be 122 percent of GDP.

This ten-year period includes only the very beginnings of the looming entitlement crisis. The national debt at the end of World War II was 113 percent of GDP. Throwing President Obama's economic policies on top of the entitlement crisis would put the national debt well past that record. House GOP budget chief Paul Ryan projected that even before Obamacare the national debt would reach 200 percent of GDP by 2035 and continue rocketing upwards.

The annual deficit by 2020 would still be well over $1 trillion ($1.253) and rising, according to the new CBO figures. Net interest spending would have quadrupled by then to $916 billion for the year, 27 percent more than we spend today for national defense and 34 percent more than the defense spending Obama proposes for 2015. Indeed, that is almost the same as what the Obama budget would spend on Medicare in 2020, effectively adding another entitlement program the size of Medicare.

All this was the budget outlook before adoption of the Patient Protection and Affordable Care Act. In the face of this long-term entitlement crisis, it could not be more fiscally reckless and irresponsible to adopt a new entitlement for middle- and upper-income households and to sharply expand existing entitlements for low-income families.

4. Conclusion

The federal debt is so enormous, and forecasts of its growth are so frightening, that many people simply refuse to think about it. Obama and the Democrats in Congress took advantage of this willful ignorance to pass legislation that threatens the country's very survival.

An analysis by *USA Today* put the burden at $546,668 per family in 2008, "quadruple what the average U.S. household owes for all mortgages, car loans, credit cards and other debt combined."[177] The amount jumped by $55,000 from 2007 to 2008, a 12 percent increase due to "an explosion of federal borrowing during the recession, plus an aging population driving up the costs of Medicare and Social Security."

Obamacare will contribute to doubling this per-capita debt in four years and quadruple it by 2020. Your family's share of the national debt will be more than $1 million in 2012, and nearly $4 million in 2020. Even these estimates are likely too low.

No one who is serious can look at numbers like these and believe Obamacare was a good idea. Either the law is repealed, or the nation will be bankrupt in a decade. The math really is that simple.

Part 6

Broken Promises

Besides the broken promises regarding health costs discussed in Part 2, and taxes in Part 4, and deficits in Part 5, Obamacare breaks at least three other promises made by candidate Barack Obama. See if you remember these.

1. No, You Can't Keep Your Current Health Plan

President Obama pledged that under his health care legislation, "If you like your health care plan, you can keep your health care plan. Period."[178] But that won't be true if your employer drops your insurance coverage under the incentives created by Obamacare. The government's own Centers for Medicare & Medicaid Services estimates 14 million people will lose their employer-provided coverage as a result of the Act.[179] More realistic is the estimate by former CBO Director Douglas Holtz-Eakin that 43 million will lose their employer-provided coverage.

Obamacare may end up forcing many more employers to drop their current plans. On June 14, the Obama administration released proposed new regulations under the Act indicating the narrow circumstances under which current employer plans would be considered in compliance with the new Act, a provision called "grandfathering." *The New York Times* reported, "In issuing the rules, the Administration said ... allowing people 'to keep their current coverage if they like it'" was "just one goal of the legislation."[180] *The Times* reported about half of all current employer-provided plans will likely fail to meet Obamacare standards by the end of 2013,[181] which would mean about 87 million workers would lose their current plan. That would include as many as 80 percent of those working for small businesses, the administration itself projects.[182]

Industry sources are even more skeptical that employers will keep grandfathered plans. A plan does not qualify if the employer changes the employer contribution by more than 5 percent, or changes insurance carriers even if the exact same benefits are provided. The Act imposes huge administrative burdens on insurers who choose to continue to administer grandfathered plans, since, for example, the same policy would have two different sets of benefits depending on if it was purchased on March 22, 2010, or March 24, 2010. Some insurance carriers have already announced they will not allow plan changes in the individual market because of the administrative complexity.

Obamacare may force many employers to drop their current plans as well by imposing penalties on those who charge premiums in excess of 9.5 percent of an employee's household income. According to the health benefits consulting firm Mercer, nearly 40 percent of employers would be subject to that penalty with their current plans.[183] Given that and the difficulties for employers in determining the household incomes for each of their employees, many employers are likely to drop their current plan for a cheaper, less-costly alternative, or drop their employer-provided insurance altogether.

You also will not be able to keep your current health plan if your insurer terminates current insurance offerings, or goes out of business altogether, as is quite possible when the costly mandates of Obamacare collide with the extreme political pressures against premium increases.

Many seniors won't be able to keep their current health plans either. The Act includes $145 billion in cuts to Medicare Advantage health plans.[184] About one-fourth of all seniors have chosen their Medicare coverage to be provided through these plans. The Centers for Medicare & Medicaid Services estimates 7.4 million seniors will lose their Medicare Advantage insurance by 2017, about half of all seniors with Medicare Advantage at that time.[185]

Who gets to keep their current health plans? Very few people indeed. This promise is obviously broken.

2. No, You Can't Keep Your Current Doctor

The president also has famously promised that under his health care takeover, "If you like your doctor, you will be able to keep your doctor, period."[186] But especially for seniors on Medicare, where doctors and hospitals face trillions of dollars in cuts in payments for their services, the real question is whether your doctor will be willing to keep you.

Many doctors are likely to terminate their Medicare practices or at least refuse to see new Medicare patients. For many seniors, this will be an even bigger problem in regard to specialists they have come to know and expect to rely on. Rationing of care to seniors necessarily means they won't be able to see their current doctors as frequently ... or at all.

As resources are constricted throughout the health care system, less access to doctors and specialists will become a problem for all Americans. Spending controls and reduced reimbursement levels will mean less investment in medical facilities and equipment, meaning fewer doctors' appointments and longer waits for care. Because of reduced payments and loss of freedom to control their own practices, doctors will retire early or leave their practice for other professional opportunities. New doctors will tend to be employees of hospitals and big networks, and they will work fewer hours and see (briefly) a far greater number of patients than doctors did in the past.

It's simply an insult to the intelligence of voters for President Obama and Democrats in Congress to continue to claim that access to doctors won't be drastically reduced by the legislation they have passed. Another Obama promise will be broken.

3. No, this Will Not Spur an Economic Recovery

Another theme consistently reiterated by President Obama is that his health plan was essential to restoring long-term economic growth. But Obamacare in fact will slash jobs, wages, and economic growth.

Obamacare's employer mandate will impose a costly new burden on employers, raising the cost of labor and consequently causing them to reduce wages or the size of their workforces. A study by the National Federation of Independent Business (NFIB) concludes the Obamacare employer mandate would eliminate 1.6 million jobs by 2014, two-thirds in small businesses.[187] That would add an extra percentage point to the unemployment rate, with more job losses and higher unemployment to come over the longer run.

President Obama touts the Small Business Tax Credit as helping to finance the cost of employer-provided insurance for small businesses.[188] But the provisions of that credit will only further discourage employment and reduce wages. Only firms with ten employees or fewer that pay their workers $25,000 or less on average qualify for the full credit, with the credit phasing down to zero for firms with more than 25 employees and as the firm's average wage rises to $50,000. This effectively works as a penalty on small businesses for creating more jobs, hiring more workers, and paying better wages. Only 12 percent of small businesses will qualify for the credit, and even then, it is available only for a maximum of six years.[189]

Another study by former CBO Director Douglas Holtz-Eakin focuses on the effect of Obamacare's health insurance subsidies on wages, income, and work.[190] Because the subsidy phases out as income rises, it acts as an effective tax on higher wages and incomes. For a two-earner family with two children, the result is to roughly double the effective marginal tax rate in the income tax code for workers making more than about $65,000 a year. Like all marginal tax rate increases, this discourages higher wages, incomes and work, and any efforts to become more productive. As Holtz-Eakin explains,

> Thus, for every additional worker that faces a loss in employer coverage we have an additional worker who faces a greater difficulty in getting ahead when taking an extra shift, finding a way for a second parent to work, or investing in night school courses to qualify for a raise. Additional work will mean handing the government as much as 41 percent of the additional income earned.[191]

Further reducing jobs, wages, and economic growth is Obamacare's additional 3.8 percent tax on investment income from capital gains, dividends, interest, and in other forms. This adds to the negative effects of the expiration of the Bush tax cuts in 2011, together raising the top capital gains rate by nearly 60 percent and the top dividends tax rate by nearly 200 percent. That will sharply discourage the capital investment necessary to create jobs, resulting in higher unemployment. The loss of capital also means lower productivity, which means lower wages. Overall, this translates into lower economic growth.

4. Conclusion

Politicians make promises all the time, and their record of keeping them is poor. Candidate Obama, though, said he was different. The "hope" and "change" he promised were a break from the posturing and cynicism of politics past and an embrace of dialogue and bipartisan consensus-building. Many voters took this promise seriously and cast their votes for him.

The reality of Obamacare stands in stark contrast to the promises of the candidate, now president. Who can read or listen to recordings of the president promising to protect people's right to keep their current health plans and doctors, and then read the language of the Act – his legislation – that so obviously violates that promise, and not feel the president was being untruthful?

Part 7

The Path Not Taken

America should, of course, provide a safety net so no one suffers due to lack of essential health care. But that can be accomplished without any of the big-government components of Obamacare. Indeed, done right, it can be accomplished while expanding the power and control of patients over their own health care and actually reducing rather than enlarging government's role in health care.[192]

The alternative reform plan described below would involve repealing all 159 new bureaucracies, agencies, boards, commissions, and programs created by Obamacare. It would reduce federal spending and taxes by at least $1 trillion and reduce future deficits sharply as well. It would reform Medicaid into a voucher program that would dramatically improve health care for the poor. It would eliminate counterproductive, costly, and unnecessary regulations, thereby reducing costs and expanding freedom of choice for everyone.

Because of all of the problems created by Obamacare, the misshapen legislation is just the beginning, not the end, of the battle to reform health care policy in America. Obamacare is so fundamentally wrong-headed that it takes us in the opposite direction of the essential reforms that are needed. Perhaps such a disastrously wrong step was necessary to reveal the path not taken. That path is discussed here.

1. A Health Care Safety Net

President Obama and the Democrats pursued the health policy debate as if the Medicaid program, already consuming close to $500 billion per year in government spending on health care for the poor, did not exist. But fundamental reform of that Medicaid program would provide the foundation for a comprehensive health care safety net.

Medicaid reform should be based on the successful 1996 reform of the old Aid to Families with Dependent Children (AFDC) welfare program.[193] That reform sent the federal share of spending for the program back to each state in a finite block grant, with each state then to create a new welfare program focused on getting recipients back to work. Under the old program's matching-funds formula, the federal government sent states more money the more they spent, which encouraged states to enroll people in AFDC welfare. The new fixed federal block grant did not vary with the amount of state spending. If costs for the program rose in a state, the state would have to pay for the added costs itself. If the state saved money through innovation and finding work for those on the welfare rolls, the state could keep the savings.

This reform transformed the incentives for state bureaucrats running the programs, with spectacular results. Welfare rolls dropped from 12.2 million in 1996 to 4.1 million in 2006, a national decline of 67 percent.[194]

Medicaid reform should follow that model. The current matching-funds formula should be replaced with finite block grants, adjusted each year for health care inflation, to be used for a completely redesigned Medicaid program in each state. Under such a reform, states could better serve the poor by using the program to provide vouchers for the purchase of private health insurance, enabling the poor to use the same hospitals, clinics, and doctors the non-poor do.

Armed with vouchers, poor families would be free to choose the health insurance coverage they prefer, including high-deductible plans with health savings accounts discussed below. This would enable them to escape the low-quality coverage and care of the current Medicaid ghetto, which underpays doctors and hospitals so severely for the services they provide to the poor that nationally one-third do not accept any Medicaid patients, and many of the rest limit the number they will treat.[195] This leaves the poor on Medicaid often suffering disabling difficulties in obtaining essential health care.

Each state's voters would be free to decide how much assistance for the purchase of health insurance they wanted to provide at what income levels. Reforms that would increase the quality of care while lowering costs, which state lawmakers and bureaucrats currently have little incentive to consider, could finally get the attention they deserve.[196] The poor would be assured of enough assistance to purchase at least basic, essential, health insurance, so no one would have to go uninsured for lack of money to buy health insurance. This would help the middle-income as well, by reducing the cost-shifting that results now because Medicaid so badly underpays doctors and hospitals.

2. State High-Risk Pools

Another component of a complete health care safety net would be state high-risk pools. The majority of states already have such pools, and they work quite well.[197] Persons who cannot obtain health insurance because of their health condition are typically eligible for coverage through the state's risk pool and are charged premiums that are subsidized by a tax on insurance companies or by general tax revenues.

Few people become truly uninsurable because of a health condition. But trying to force those who do into the same insurance market as everyone else, through such regulations as guaranteed issue and community rating, just ruins health insurance for the general public, making it too expensive and sharply increasing the number of people who choose to go without insurance as a result. Providing for the uninsurable separately through their own pool is a much better policy.

High-risk pools address the problem of pre-existing conditions as well. Most insurers limit coverage for pre-existing conditions for only a few months. Each state's high-risk pool could provide coverage for pre-existing conditions during those excluded months, or for however long is necessary to get coverage for that condition.

High-risk pools are not without their critics.[198] Most of the criticism focuses on the lack of financing for the pools, which forces fund managers to enforce tight restrictions and caps on enrollments, raise cost-sharing, and minimize marketing outreach to the uninsured. The cost of expanding high-risk pools to address these concerns would be tiny compared to the costs of the Obama health plan.

Obamacare provides for setting up such a risk pool in every state next year,[199] recognizing to a degree the desirability of the idea. But the president's legislation would eliminate these pools in 2014, folding everyone into the state exchanges instead. This is bad policy. The risk pools should be permanent, with the states each free to design and run them as they prefer, without the unnecessary federal control in Obamacare.

The federal role should be limiting to ensuring that state risk pools are adequately funded. The pools should work in conjunction with Medicaid so that those without funds to pay risk pool premiums would receive Medicaid vouchers to do so. This would provide a much lower cost solution to the problems of people with pre-existing conditions who have not previously obtained coverage.

Newt Gingrich has proposed complementing high-risk pools with health plans that specialize in managing care for the sick with costly chronic diseases.[200] Such special-needs plans actively compete in Medicare Advantage to cover the sickest Medicare beneficiaries. Instead of eviscerating Medicare Advantage as Obamacare does, the role of these plans should be expanded in Medicare, Medicaid, and in employer and individual coverage.

3. Consumer Protections

A third component of a comprehensive health care safety net involves what is usually called consumer protection, but is actually only sound, fundamental principles of law. In a town hall meeting in New Hampshire last summer, President Obama said that under his health plan,

> [I]nsurance companies ... will not be able to drop your coverage if you get sick. They will not be able to water down your coverage when you need it. Your health insurance should be there for you when it counts – not just when you're paying premiums, but when you actually get sick. And it will be when we pass this plan.[201]

But dropping or watering-down your health insurance coverage after you get sick has long been illegal in America, and it should be. Health insurance that can be cut off after you get sick is, as explained in Part 2, like fire insurance that can be cut off after your house catches fire. That is not health insurance, it is fraud, because it would not be protecting you against unexpected health costs, or anything.

The prohibition against this fraud, already on the books in all 50 states, was nationalized in the Health Insurance Portability and Accountability Act (HIPAA) of 1996. That legislation even provided that if you lose employer-provided health insurance coverage for any reason (changing jobs, layoffs, employer goes out of business, divorce) any private insurer you apply to within two months must take you, regardless of health condition. That is workable because such individuals are not trying to game the system, waiting until they are sick before they buy guaranteed coverage, but are actually trying to responsibly maintain continuous coverage.

The law in America has also long provided for what has been termed guaranteed renewability, which means as long as you continue to pay your premiums, the insurance company cannot cut you off because you get sick, nor can it impose premium increases any greater than for anyone else in your original risk pool.

There may still be some loopholes in the employer group market that should be closed, but by campaigning on people's fear of losing their health insurance, candidate and then President Obama was trying to take credit for solving a problem that had already been solved for the vast majority of Americans. Whatever loopholes may have needed closing did not require the massive government takeover of health care he advocated and eventually signed into law.

4. Consumer Choice Tax Credits

Since World War II, employer-provided health insurance has been exempt from federal income taxes, while health insurance purchased by individuals has not been. Reformers have long advocated extending the tax preference to everyone, including the unemployed, self-employed, and people whose employers don't offer health insurance benefits.

Expanding the tax preference to all buyers of health insurance can and should be done on a revenue-neutral basis by limiting the value of the preference for people receiving the most generous insurance benefits and who are in the highest tax brackets. The current system acts as a windfall for them, subsidizing by hundreds of billions of dollars a year people who don't really need the help.[202] The better idea is to include the value of employer-provided health insurance in taxable income, but then everyone should receive a refundable tax credit of a flat amount, good for the purchase of health insurance whether obtained through an employer or otherwise.

An example of this reform idea is the health insurance tax credit included by Rep. Paul Ryan (R-WI) in his "A Roadmap for America's Future," a series of reforms to solve the entitlement crisis.[203] That plan would provide $2,300 for individuals and $5,700 for families for the purchase of health insurance. This would not pay for all the costs of such insurance, but it is enough to make insurance affordable for all but the poor and uninsured people with serious pre-existing conditions. When combined with the Medicaid vouchers and high-risk pools, the health insurance tax credit provides a complete solution to the nation's health insurance access problem.

The consumer choice tax credit idea has some additional advantages. Employees would each be free to choose the health insurance coverage they prefer, rather than being stuck with the health insurance chosen for them by their employer. Employee-purchased insurance would be the property of the individual worker and therefore completely portable. The price of insurance premiums would become plainly visible to the individuals who benefit from the insurance, which will help offset some of the incentive to over-consume when third parties foot most or all of the bill.

Consumer choice tax credits should replace Obamacare's health insurance subsidies. That would result in an enormous savings to taxpayers. Since the tax credits cost no more than the current tax exemption for employer-provided health insurance, the savings would equal the entire cost of the Obamacare health insurance subsidies under the Act, at least $500 billion in the first six years, and probably more than $1 trillion based on the earlier analysis of likely spending trends.

5. Health Savings Accounts

The creation of medical savings accounts in 1993, superceded by health savings accounts (HSAs) in 2003, represented a major step forward in the effort to empower individuals rather than government in the health care arena. Individuals with HSAs keep most of their money for health care in a savings account, earning tax-free interest, with the rest going to purchase a high-deductible insurance policy. The premium cost for such catastrophic coverage, with deductibles generally ranging from $2,000 to $6,000 a year, is much lower than for standard, low-deductible health insurance, allowing the savings in the account to grow quickly to cover the entire deductible.

Patients with HSAs are free to use the money in their accounts for any health care product or service they choose, including preventive care, check-ups, prescriptions, dental care, eye care, and the full range of alternative medicine. Payment for these goods and services comes directly from the HSAs, which have their own checkbooks or debit cards, with no pre-approval by insurers necessary. Nothing can do more to put patients in control of their own health care. All non-catastrophic health care is completely under the patient's control.

HSAs restore powerful market incentives to control costs.[204] Patients are using their own money for non-catastrophic care. That means they will avoid overly costly or unnecessary care and look for doctors and hospitals that can provide them quality care at lower cost, creating real market competition to reduce costs. Money kept in HSAs can be used for health care in later years, or for anything in retirement.

Participation in high-deductible insurance plans has been soaring in recent years. The number of Americans with an HSA or similar high-deductible plan increased by 43 percent from 2006 to 2007, 35 percent from 2007 to 2008, and 31 percent from 2008 to 2009.[205] The latest numbers show another increase of 25 percent from January 2009 to January 2010.[206] Coverage in the large group market rose by 33 percent from 2009 to 2010, and in the small group market by 22 percent.[207] The National Health Interview Survey (NHIS) conducted by the federal government's Centers for Disease Control and Prevention found that in 2009 about 23 percent of the privately insured population was covered by HSAs, HRAs, or similar high-deductible health plans,[208] which may have exceeded HMO enrollment that year.[209] Almost 50 percent of those with private insurance obtained outside their employment were covered by such high-deductible plans.[210] Funds held in HSAs totaled more than $9.2 billion in 2009 and were projected to grow to more than $16 billion by the end of 2010.[211]

HSAs and similar high-deductible plans have been proven to reduce costs. Premiums in 2009 for those aged 30 to 54 in the individual market averaged $2,465 a year for singles and $5,335 for a family.[212] In the group market, family premiums averaged nearly 25 percent less than the standard charge of more than $12,000 per family, with average premiums for singles at $3,691 in the large group market and $3,944 in the small group market.[213] Moreover, premium increases for such employer plans have averaged 50 percent less than the market standard, including for federal employees in the Federal Employees Health Benefits Program, with no increase at all for many such plans in recent years.[214]

In stark contrast to the failure of the Massachusetts plan, HSAs reduce emergency room use. A study by Regence Blue Shield found patients reduced their use of emergency rooms by 32 percent after switching to HSA coverage.[215] A 2007 study published in the *Journal of the American Medical Association* found similar results, documenting that patients paying with their own HSA funds avoid emergency rooms for routine, non-severe conditions.[216]

Policymakers should consider reforms that make HSAs more attractive to everyone. Limits on deposits into the accounts should be raised, and restrictions on how funds can be spent – such as Obamacare's exclusion of non-prescription drugs – should be avoided or repealed. High-deductible plans with HSAs should be made the default insurance option for public-sector employees. If the reforms described earlier are adopted, workers should be allowed to use their consumer choice tax credits to choose high-deductible plans with HSAs, and those on Medicaid should be free to use their vouchers for such coverage as well. Medicare should ultimately be transformed entirely into a Medicare Advantage system, with seniors free to use Medicare vouchers for the purchase of any private health plan they choose, including those with health savings accounts.

6. Further Consumer-Based Reforms

Additional reforms would complete what I've called "the path not taken."[217] They include the following:

- *Repeal unnecessary regulations.* Considerable progress can be made toward making health insurance more affordable simply by repealing existing regulations that are unnecessary and counterproductive. They include mandated benefits, guaranteed issue and community rating, certificate of need, rate regulations, unreasonable clean claims and prompt pay laws, and regulations on PPOs.

- *Allow interstate sale of health insurance.* State regulation of health insurers has resulted in steep barriers to entry in each state and prohibitions on consumers purchasing out-of-state insurance. Costs would decline if consumers could buy insurance across state lines and if insurers could market their products nationally. States also would come under pressure to repeal costly and unnecessary coverage mandates.

- *Encourage medical entrepreneurship.* Federal and state regulations can be revised to reduce barriers to the opening of retail health clinics, specialty hospitals, medical tourism, and telemedicine. These innovations promise to expand supply and reduce costs.

- *Medical malpractice liability reform.* Traditional tort standards for medical liability should be strictly enforced. Doctors and hospitals should be responsible only for damages for which they were the proximate cause. Non-economic damages, such as compensation for pain and suffering, should be limited. Punitive damages should apply only in criminal proceedings, not in civil trials.

- *Allow association insurance.* People should be free to band together for the purpose of purchasing health insurance. Such associations can spread risk and have bargaining power similar to what large employers have.

- *Encourage the creation of private exchanges.* Small, medium, and large businesses, trade associations, and civic associations should be able to set up their own market-based insurance exchanges to offer their employees and members a wide range of possible insurance alternatives. Employers could offer their workers a defined contribution payment towards any of the health plans on the exchange. This would encourage more employers to offer health coverage to their workers, leading to greater coverage and reduced numbers of uninsured.

7. Conclusion

All of the cost and heavy-handed government control of health care that will occur under the Patient Protection and Affordable Care Act – the 159 new government bureaucracies, agencies, boards, and commissions ruling health care, the trillions of dollars in Medicare cuts, the tax increases and massive deficits – all of this is completely unnecessary. The uninsured can and should be covered with modest increases in public assistance that could easily be offset by improvements in the efficiency and fairness of the health care finance system. The reforms described above would do all of this.

We have a national program to help people who cannot afford to buy private health insurance. It is called Medicaid, and it is crying out for reform. Rather than start there, Obama and the Democrats built on and around that flawed program, erecting a huge new infrastructure of rules and bureaucracies, all to address problems that wouldn't exist if current rules and bureaucracies weren't failing.

We can expand high-risk pools to take care of middle- and upper-income people with pre-existing conditions who cannot find affordable health insurance. We can redirect the hundreds of billions of dollars already used to subsidize employer-provided health insurance to target that aid to people who truly need help: the uninsured, the self-employed, and people whose employers don't provide health insurance benefits. We can motivate people to prioritize their use of health care services and become careful consumers of services by expanding the use of health savings accounts.

These reforms, and others described here, are hardly radical or new. They have been part of the reform agenda of scholars and experts for many years. They were wrongly dismissed by Obama and the Democrats in their quest to expand government authority over this vitally important part of the American economy and of the lives of voters.

This missed opportunity is perhaps the biggest disaster of Obamacare. An opportunity to genuinely fix America's health care system was squandered. Time and energy that could have been devoted to moving ahead will now have to be spent undoing a major mistake.

Conclusion

Danny Williams, age 60, is the premier of Newfoundland, in Canada, the land of "single payer" national health insurance. When he needed heart surgery, he snuck into the U.S. to get it. As Grace-Marie Turner reported in February 2010, Williams told reporters after his surgery, "This was my heart, my choice, and my health. I did not sign away my right to get the best possible health care for myself when I entered politics."[218] That best possible health care was at Mount Sinai Medical Center in Miami, Florida.

Why Williams felt he had to come to America was further illuminated by the recent heart surgery of former president Bill Clinton. As Dr. Marc Siegel explained in the *New York Post*,

> Clinton, of course, got the best of care – a cardiac stent (a tiny metal cylinder) coated with a drug to help keep his artery open. Recent studies in the *New England Journal of Medicine* and elsewhere have shown that these drug-eluting stents are more effective than bare metal ones. But they cost two-to-four times more – and the technology is relatively new. That combination has left government-run health-care systems slow to adopt them. ... Per capita, our neighbors to the North receive only half as many coronary [operations]. And only 30 percent of the stents placed in Canada are drug-eluting, compared to a whopping 80 percent in the United States. So a Canadian cardiac patient is less than a quarter as likely as an American to be outfitted with the kind of state-of-the-art stent that Clinton had. In Canada, land of single payer health insurance, you're also less likely to get the stent as soon as the need is clear.[219]

When their own lives are at risk, even advocates of single-payer health care suddenly understand what is at stake. America today enjoys the best, most advanced health care in the world. That is why so many come here from all those countries with national health insurance, or "universal" health care, to get their essential care. But this is exactly what will now be lost under the Patient Protection and Affordable Care Act

This *Heartland Policy Study* has explained how Obamacare represents nothing less than a government takeover of health care in America. It will cause spending to skyrocket, care to be rationed, and taxes and government deficits to rise. It breaks all the promises candidate and then President Obama made about access to care, taxes, and the deficit. And it was all unnecessary: Much simpler reforms could have been adopted providing for a complete health care safety net, ensuring that everyone will have access to essential health care. Real health care reform would provide maximum power, control, and choice to patients and the doctors they have chosen for their health care. The key to making that work is not more government control and spending, but reforms that provide patients with market incentives to control the costs of their care, eliminating all forms of third-party health care rationing.

Obamacare is a disaster. Rather than liberate the American health care system from bureaucracy and waste, it blankets it with more of both, suffocating innovation and destroying freedom. The result is a system that is inconsistent with the freedom, prosperity, high living standards, and traditions of the American people.

Endnotes

1 Nancy Pelosi, "Pelosi Remarks at the 2010 Legislative Conference for National Association of Counties," March 9, 2010, http://www.speaker.gov/newsroom/pressreleases?id=1576.

2 Peter Ferrara, "The Obama Health Plan: Rationing, Higher Taxes, and Lower Quality Health Care," *Heartland Policy Study* No. 123, The Heartland Institute, August 2009.

3 John Goodman and Gerald Musgrave, *Patient Power: Solving America's Health Care Crisis* (Washington, DC: Cato Institute,1992); Peter J. Ferrara, "More Than A Theory: Medical Savings Accounts At Work," *Policy Analysis* No. 220, Cato Institute, March 14, 1995; Peter J. Ferrara, "Medicare and the Private Sector," *Yale Law and Policy Review,* Volume VI, No. 1, 1988.

4 Newt Gingrich, *To Save America* (New York: Regnery Publishing, 2010), p. 87.

5 Patient Protection and Affordable Care Act (PPACA), Sections 6301, 6302, 3001, 3007, 3011-3015.

6 PPACA, Sections 2702, 2705.

7 PPACA, Section 2704.

8 PPACA, Section 2701.

9 PPACA, Section 2713.

10 PPACA, Section 2711.

11 PPACA, Sections 1301, 1302, 2707, 2711, 2713, 2714 .

12 PPACA, Sections 2714, 2702, 2705.

13 PPACA, Section 2701.

14 PPACA, Section 1302.

15 PPACA, Sections 1341, 1343.

16 PPACA, Section 1501.

17 PPACA, Section 1302.

18 PPACA, Section 1302.

19 PPACA, Sections 1511, 1513.

20 PPACA, Sections 1401, 1402.

21 PPACA, Sections 2001, 2003.

22 Richard S. Foster, chief actuary, Centers for Medicare & Medicaid Services, "Estimated Financial Effects of the 'Patient Protection and Affordable Care Act,' as Amended," April 22, 2010, p. 6, Table 2.

23 PPACA, Sections 1311, 1312, 1322.

24 PPACA, Section 1302.

25 Barack Obama, "Remarks by the President to a Joint Session of Congress on Health Care," The White House, September 9, 2009.

26 Barack Obama, "Cutting Costs and Covering America: A 21st Century Health Care System," Speech at University of Iowa, May 29, 2007; Gingrich, supra note 4, p. 93.

27 Foster, supra note 22.

28 PPACA, Sections 2001, 2002, 2003.

29 Foster, supra note 22.

30 Douglas Holtz-Eakin and Cameron Smith, "Labor Markets and Health Care Reform: New Results," American Action Forum, May 2010, p. 2.

31 Ibid.

32 Douglas W. Elmendorf, Congressional Budget Office, "Letter to the Honorable Nancy Pelosi," March 20, 2010, Table 2.

33 Foster, supra note 22, p. 5, Table 1.

34 PPACA, Section 1302.

35 Janet Adamy, "White House Unveils Free Preventative Services," *The Wall Street Journal,* July 15, 2010.

36 PPACA, Section 2713.

37 G.A. Jensen and M. Morrisey, "Mandated Benefit Laws and Employer-Sponsored Health Insurance," Health Insurance Association of America, 1999.

38 PPACA, Section 2711.

39 PPACA, Sections 2702, 2704, 2705.

40 Conrad F. Meier, *Destroying Insurance Markets* (Washington, DC and Chicago, IL: Council for Affordable Health Insurance and The Heartland Institute, 2005); Leigh Wachenheim and Hans Leida, "The Impact of Guaranteed Issue and Community Rating Reforms on Individual Insurance Markets," Milliman, Inc., July 10, 2007; Merrill Mathews, "Should We Abandon Risk Assessment in Health Insurance," *Issues and Answers* No. 154, Council for Affordable Health Insurance, May 2009; Devon Herrick, "The Folly of Health Insurance Mandates," *Brief Analysis* No. 652, National Center for Policy Analysis, April 9, 2009.

41 AHIP Center for Policy and Research, *Individual Health Insurance 2009: A Comprehensive Survey of Premiums, Availability, and Benefits,* October 2009, pp. 4, 6.

42 PriceWaterhouseCoopers, "Potential Impact of Health Reform on the Cost of Private Health Insurance Coverage," October 2009.

43 Wellpoint, Inc., "Impact of Health Reform on Premiums," October 2009.

44 Merrill Mathews, "Should We Abandon Risk Assessment in Health Insurance?" *Issues and Answers* No. 154, Council for Affordable Health Insurance, May 2009.

45 Grace-Marie Turner and Tara Persico, "Massachusetts' Health Reform Plan: Miracle or Muddle?" Galen Institute, July 2009, p. 3.

46 Ibid., p. 8.

47 Michael Tanner, "Massachusetts Miracle or Massachusetts Miserable: What the Failure of the 'Massachusetts Model' Tells Us about Health Care Reform," *Briefing Papers* No. 112, Cato Institute, June 9, 2009, p. 1.

48 Ibid., p. 6; Turner, supra note 45, p. 3.

49 Greg Scandlen, "Three Lessons from Massachusetts," National Center for Policy Analysis, *Brief Analysis* No. 667, July 28, 2009.

50 Ibid.; Sally C. Pipes, "Mass Health Meltdown Is Your Future," Pacific Research Institute, May 25, 2010.

51 Turner, supra note 45, p. 7.

52 Aaron Yelowitz and Michael F. Cannon, "The Massachusetts Health Plan: Much Pain, Little Gain," *Policy Analysis* No. 657, Cato Institute, January 2010, p. 10.

53 Tanner, supra note 47, p. 4.

54 Scandlen, supra note 49, p. 1.

55 Ibid.

56 Tanner, supra note 47, p. 5.

57 "The Massachusetts Health Mess," *The Wall Street Journal,* July 11, 2009; Kevin Wrege, "The Bay State Games," CAHI's Health Care Reform Central, Council for Affordable Health Insurance, July 16, 2009.

58 Grace-Marie Turner, "The Failure of RomneyCare," *The Wall Street Journal,* March 17, 2010.

59 Elmendorf, supra note 32, Table 2.

60 PPACA, Sections 9001, 10901.

61 PPACA, Sections 9010, 10905.

62 Elmendorf, supra note 32, Table 2.

63 PPACA, Section 9008.

64 PPACA, Sections 9009, 10904.

65 Foster, supra note 22, Table 3.

66 Gingrich, supra note 4, p. 92.

67 Will Fox, FSA, MAAA, and John Pickering, FSA, .MAAA, "Hospital and Physician Cost Shift: Payment Level Comparison of Medicare, Medicaid, and Commercial Payers," Milliman, Inc., December 2008; see also, Turner, p. 10.

68 John Boehner, "ObamaCare: Three Months of Broken Promises," June 23, 2010, pp. 4-6, http://gopleader.gov/UploadedFiles/ObamaCare3MonthsBrokenPromises.pdf.

69 James Rowley and Kristin Jensen, "Health-Care Plans Fail to Curtail Spending, CBO Says," Bloomberg, July 16, 2009.

70 Senate Budget Committee, Minority Staff, "Budget Perspective: The Real Deficit Effect of the Democrats' Health Package," March 23, 2010.

71 The chief actuary of Medicare already projects that 15 percent of the doctors, hospitals, surgeons, and specialists providing medical care and health services to seniors under Medicare will become unprofitable and have to close as a result of these cuts. Foster, supra note 22, p. 10.

72 David Olmos, "Mayo Clinic in Arizona to Stop Treating Some Medicare Patients," Bloomberg, December 31, 2009.

73 Foster, supra note 22, p. 10.

74 "The War on Specialists," *The Wall Street Journal,* editorial, October 6, 2009.

75 John C. Goodman and Gerald L. Musgrave, "A Primer on Managed Competition," *NCPA Policy Report* No. 183, National Center for Policy Analysis, April 1994.

76 Alain Enthoven, "The History and Principles of Managed Competition," *Health Affairs,* 1993 Supplement, p. 35.

77 Scott Gottlieb, "No, You Can't Keep Your Health Plan," *The Wall Street Journal,* May 18, 2010.

78 PPACA, Sections 1341, 1342, 1343.

79 Goodman and Musgrave, supra note 75.

80 Betsy McCaughey, "What the Pelosi Health-Care Bill Really Says," *The Wall Street Journal,* November 7, 2009.

81 Ibid.; PPACA, Section 1302.

82 Scott Gottlieb, "What Doctors and Patients Have to Lose Under ObamaCare," *The Wall Street Journal,* December 23, 2009.

83 Gardiner Harris, "More Doctors Giving Up Private Practices," *The New York Times,* March 25, 2010.

84 Gottlieb, supra note 82.

85 Ibid.

86 Harris, supra note 83.

87 Merrill Mathews, "America's Coming Health Care Oligopoly," Forbes.com, July 7, 2010.

88 PPACA, Sections 6301, 6302.

89 Gingrich, supra note 4, p. 91.

90 Leonard A. Zwelling, "'Comparative Effectiveness' Research Is Always Behind the Curve," *The Wall Street Journal,* March 16, 2010.

91 Ibid.

92 "A Breast Cancer Preview," *The Wall Street Journal,* editorial, November 19, 2009.

93 Dara Richardson-Heron, "Why You Should Keep Getting Mammograms," *New York Post,* November 29, 2009.

94 Betsy McCaughey, "Medical Privacy and Obamacare," *The Wall Street Journal,* April 9, 2010, p. A19.

95 President's Council of Economic Advisors, "The Economic Case for Health Reform," June 2, 2009.

96 Gingrich, supra note 4, pp. 90-91.

97 Texas Physicians Hospitals, "Federal Health Bill Analysis," March 23, 2010.

98 Ibid.

99 Peter Loftus, "Eli Lilly Sets Plans for Emerging Markets," *The Wall Street Journal,* June 8, 2010.

100 The Physicians' Foundation, "The Physician's Perspective: Medical Practice in 2008," Survey Key Findings, November 18, 2008.

101 Milton Friedman, "How to Reform Health Care," *Hoover Digest,* 2001 #3.

102 "Massachusetts Health Care Reform is a Pioneer Effort, but Complications Remain," *Annals of Internal Medicine,* American College of Physicians, March 2008, pp. 489-492; Turner, supra note 58.

103 Liz Kowalczyk, "Across Massachusetts, Wait to See Doctors Grows," *Boston Globe,* September 22, 2008; Turner, supra note 58, p. 9.

104 John Goodman, "Scaling the Summit," *Health Alert,* National Center for Policy Analysis, February 26, 2010.

105 Grace-Marie Turner and Amy Menefee, "Does Massachusetts Have a Miracle Cure for Health Reform?" March 23, 2009, http://www.galen.org/component,8/action,show_content/id,13/blog_id,1178/type,33/.

106 Grace-Marie Turner, "Dangers of Sweeping Health Reform," *The Oklahoman*, July 30, 2009.

107 Turner, supra note 58.

108 Greg Scandlen, "Three Lessons from Massachusetts," *Brief Analysis* No. 667, National Center for Policy Analysis, July 28, 2009.

109 Kay Lazar, "Costly ER Still Draws Many Now Insured," *Boston Globe,* April 24, 2009; Turner, supra note 58.

110 John Goodman, supra note 104.

111 Kowalczyk, supra note 103; Turner, supra note 58, p. 10; see also Scandlen, supra note 108, p. 2.

112 Michael Bond, "Applying the Lessons of State Health Reform," *Policy Report* No. 323, National Center for Policy Analysis, September 2009, p. 8; see also Scandlen, supra note 108, p. 2.

113 Turner, supra note 58, p. 10; Scandlen, supra note 108, p. 2.

114 Scandlen, supra note 108, p. 2.

115 Kyle Cheney, "Murphy defends insurance rate caps," State House News Service, June 11, 2010; Sally C. Pipes, "The Massachusetts Health Care Mess Is Coming Soon to the Rest of America," *Washington Examiner,* June 11, 2010.

116 Pipes, supra note 50.

117 Ibid.

118 Ibid.

119 Tanner, supra note 47, p. 7; Turner, supra note 58.

120 Pipes, supra note 115.

121 Ibid.

122 Pipes, supra note 50.

123 Pipes, supra note 115; Tanner, supra note 47, p. 7.

124 As Pipes says, "This HMOs for all approach is designed to lead to soft rationing," supra note 50; see also, Tanner, supra note 47, p. 7.

125 Nadeem Esmail, "'Too Old' for Hip Surgery," Fraser Forum, www.fraserinstitute.org, June 6, 2009; see also Ferrara, supra note 2.

126 Ibid.

127 Ibid.

128 John C. Goodman, Gerald L. Musgrave, and Devon M. Herrick, *Lives at Risk: Single Payer National Health Insurance Around the World* (Lanham, MD: Rowman & Littlefield, 2004). A 2007 study published in *Lancet Oncology* found U.S. patients fare better for 13 of 16 types of cancer studied. See David Gratzer, "American Cancer Care Beats the Rest," *The Wall Street Journal,* July 22, 2008.

129 Goodman, Musgrave, and Herrick, supra note 128.

130 N. Esmail, E. Walker, and D. Wrona, "Waiting Your Turn: Hospital Waiting Lists in Canada, 17th Edition," Vancouver: Fraser Institute, 2007.

131 M. Young and E. Butler, "Britain's Million-Year Wait," *Health Care News,* June 2002.

132 Gerald Anderson, et al., "It's the Prices, Stupid: Why the United States Is So Different from Other Countries," *Health Affairs,* May/June 2002.

133 Goodman, Musgrave, and Herrick, supra note 128.

134 Nadeem Esmail and Dominika Wrona, "Medical Technology in Canada," *Studies in Health Care Policy,* Fraser Institute, August 2008, Table 10, p. 25.

135 Ibid.

136 Council for Affordable Health Insurance, "America's Affordable Health Reform Plan: A Common-Sense Solution," 2009.

137 Donald M. Berwick, M.D., "A Transatlantic Review of the NHS at 60," address at the 60th Anniversary Celebration of the NHS, July 1, 2008, Wembly, England.

138 See Ferrara, supra note 2, pp. 14-19.

139 "Rethinking Comparative Effectiveness Research, An Interview with Dr. Donald Berwick," *Biotechnology Healthcare,* June 2009, p. 36.

140 Ibid.

141 Grace-Marie Turner, "Early Warning Signs," *Health Policy Matters,* May 7, 2010.

142 Goodman, Musgrave, and Herrick, supra note 128.

143 Senator Barack Obama, Prepared Remarks for Event in Dover, New Hampshire, September 12, 2008; John Lott, "Obama's Health Care Bill Is Not What He Promised," Fox Forum, FoxNews.com, March 29, 2010.

144 PPACA, Sections 1501, 1502.

145 This description is based on Michael D. Tanner, *Bad Medicine: A Guide to the Real Costs and Consequences of the New Health Care Law*, Cato Institute, 2010; and Ryan Ellis, "Obamacare and Taxes: The Final Tab," Americans for Tax Reform, April 5, 2010, http://www.atr.org/obamacare-taxes-final-tab-a4744#ixzz0u4f5IJjD.

146 Congressional Budget Office, "An Analysis of Health Insurance Premiums Under the Patient Protection and Affordable Care Act," Letter to the Honorable Evan Bayh, November 30, 2009.

147 American Academy of Actuaries, "Letter to The Honorable Nancy Pelosi and The Honorable Harry Reid, Re: Patient Protection and Affordable Care Act (H.R. 3590) and Affordable Health Care for America Act (H.R. 3962)," January 14, 2010, pp. 2, 4.

148 See Tanner, supra note 145, and Ellis, supra note 145.

149 Marilyn Werber Serafini, "Heartburn Over Grandfathering," NationalJournal.com, June 21, 2010.

150 Quoted in John Lott, "Obama's Health Care Bill Is Not What He Promised," Fox Forum, FoxNews.com, March 29, 2010.

151 Elmendorf, supra note 32, Table 2.

152 Tanner, supra note 145, and Ellis, supra note 145.

153 Ibid.

154 Foster, supra note 22, p. 9.

155 Elmendorf, supra note 32, Table 2.

156 Stephen Moore and Phil Kerpen, "A Capital Gains Tax Cut: The Key to Economic Recovery," *IPI Policy Report* No. 164, October 11, 2001; Dan Clifton, "The Economic and Fiscal Impact of the 2003 Tax Cut," American Shareholders Association, April 2007.

157 Jay Heflin, "Most Americans Oppose Tax Increases to Save State Jobs," thehill.com, July 7, 2010.

158 Elmendorf, supra note 32, Table 2.

159 Senate Budget Committee, Minority Staff, "Budget Perspective: The Real Deficit Effect of the Health Bill," March 18, 2010.

160 Ibid.

161 Elmendorf, supra note 32, Table 4.

162 Ibid.; see also Holtz-Eakin and Smith, supra note 30, p. 4.

163 John Goodman, "Four Trojan Horses," *Health Alert,* National Center for Policy Analysis, April 15, 2010.

164 Holtz-Eakin and Smith, supra note 30, p. 2.

165 Ibid., pp. 2-4.

166 Barack Obama, "Remarks by the President to a Joint Session of Congress on Health Care, U.S. Capitol, Washington, DC," September 9, 2009.

167 Senate Budget Committee, Minority Staff, supra note 159.

168 Foster, supra note 22, Table 3, p. 8.

169 Senate Budget Committee, Minority Staff, supra note 159.

170 Holtz-Eakin and Smith, supra note 30; see also Douglas Holtz-Eakin and Michael J. Ramlet, "The Fiscal Implications of the Patient Protection and Affordable Care Act," *Health Affairs,* forthcoming.

171 Senate Budget Committee, Minority Staff, supra note 159.

172 David Gratzer, "ObamaCare's Deficits," Forbes.com, May 3, 2010.

173 *The 2009 Annual Report of the Boards of Trustees of the Federal Hospital Insurance and Federal Supplementary Medical Insurance Trust Funds*, May 12, 2009; p. 69, Table III.B10; p. 112, Table III.C16; p. 127, Table III.C23.

174 *The 2009 Annual Report of the Board of Trustees of the Federal Old-Age and Survivors Insurance and Federal Disability Insurance Trust Funds*, May 12, 2009, pp. 62, 63, Table IV.B6. Measuring the unfunded liability as under a private pension plan that cannot count on forced contributions from others not presently participating in the system would yield an unfunded liability of $16.3 trillion for Social Security. Ibid., pp. 63, 64, Table IV.B7. This assumes in addition another $2.4 trillion in federal borrowing to make good on the Social Security bonds held by the Social Security trust.

175 Brian M. Riedl and Alison Acosta Fraser, "How to Reform Entitlement Spending: A Memo to President Elect Obama," *Special Report* No. 43, The Heritage Foundation, Washington, DC, January 13, 2009, p. 2.

176 Congressional Budget Office, "An Analysis of the President's Budgetary Proposals for Fiscal 2011," March 2010.

177 Dennis Cauchon, "Leap in U.S. Debt Hits Taxpayers with 12% More Red Ink," *USA Today,* May 29, 2009.

178 Barack Obama, "Remarks by the President at the Annual Conference of the American Medical Association, Hyatt Regency Chicago, Chicago, Illinois," June 15, 2009.

179 Foster, supra note 22.

180 Robert Pear, "New Rules Changes to Benefits," *The New York Times,* June 13, 2010.

181 Ibid.

182 Robb Mandelbaum, "Small Firms May Not Keep Current Health Plans After White House Decision," *The New York Times,* June 15, 2010.

183 Mercer, "A Third of Employers May Be Penalized for Health Coverage Deemed Unaffordable," April 27, 2010.

184 Foster, supra note 22, p. 8, Table 3.

185 Foster, supra note 22, p. 11.

186 Obama, supra note 178.

187 Michael J. Chow and Bruce D. Phillips, "Small Business Effects of a National Employer Healthcare Mandate," NFIB Research Foundation, Washington, DC, January 26, 2009.

188 PPACA, Section 1421.

189 NFIB, "Five Unaffordable Facts About the New Healthcare Law: The Patient Protection and Affordable Care Act, n.d., http://www.uschamber.com/NR/rdonlyres/eyl6vl53nebj64n2rv32ny4bmluiqgrfhdz5uysmeytoxaj6vplh6onhkuwzv3hcjabx46t4kg7h52yfmkl5gsa52xg/unaffordable_+facts_healthcare.pdf.

190 Holtz-Eakin and Smith, supra note 30.

191 Ibid., p. 5.

192 See Goodman and Musgrave, supra note 3, and Ferrara, supra note 3.

193 Gary MacDougal, Kate Campaigne, and Dane Wendell, *Welfare Reform After Ten Years: A State-by-State Analysis,* The Heartland Institute, 2009.

194 Ibid.

195 Devon Herrick, "Exposing the Myths of Universal Health Coverage," *Brief Analysis* No. 651, National Center for Policy Analysis, April 9, 2009.

196 For example, see John C. Goodman, "Ten Steps to Reforming Medicaid," *Health Care News,* July 2008, and John C. Goodman et al., *Handbook on State Health Care Reform,* National Center for Policy Analysis, 2008.

197 J.P. Wieske and Merrill Matthews, "Understanding the Uninsured and What to Do about Them," Council for Affordable Health Insurance, 2007; NASCHIP, *Comprehensive Health Insurance for High-Risk Individuals: A State-by-State Analysis, 22nd Edition, 2008-2009,* Denver, 2008.

198 See L. Achman and D. Chollet, "Insuring the Uninsurable: An Overview of State High-Risk Health Insurance Pools," The Commonwealth Fund, August 2001.

199 PPACA, Section 1101. Because of inadequate funding and excessively burdensome federal regulation for these pools under the Act, 19 states have opted not to participate in them. Grace-Marie Turner, "States Face Their First Obamacare Test, *The Wall Street Journal,* April 29, 2010.

200 Gingrich, supra note 4, p. 207.

201 Barack Obama, "President Barack Obama, New Hampshire Town Hall on Health Care, Portsmouth, New Hampshire," August 11, 2009.

202 Mark V. Pauly, John C. Goodman, Judith Feder, Larry Levitt, Stuart M. Butler, David M. Cutler, and Gail R. Wilensky, "Incremental Steps Toward Health System Reform," *Health Affairs,* Spring 1995.

203 Paul Ryan, "A Roadmap for America's Future," http://www.roadmap.republicans.budget.house.gov/UploadedFiles/Roadmap2Final2.pdf.

204 Greg Scandlen, "Ten Ways Consumer Driven Health Care Is a Proven Success," *Policy Study* No. 125, The Heartland Institute, January 2010.

205 America's Health Insurance Plans (AHIP), "January 2009 Census Shows 8 Million People Covered by HSA/High Deductible Plans," May 2009.

206 America's Health Insurance Plans (AHIP), "January 2010 Census Shows 10 Million People Covered by HSA/High Deductible Plans," May 2010.

207 Ibid.

208 Michael E. Martinez and Robin E. Cohen, "Health Insurance Coverage: Early Release of Estimates from the National Health Interview Survey, January – June 2009," Centers for Disease Control and Prevention, http:/www.cdc.gov/nchs/data/nhis/earlyrelease/insur200912.htm.

209 Scandlen, supra note 204, p. 12.

210 Martinez and Cohen, supra note 208.

211 Scandlen, supra note 204, p. 6.

212 AHIP, supra note 206, p. 7.

213 Ibid., pp. 8-9.

214 Scandlen, supra note 204, p. 5.

215 "Consumer-Directed Health Plans: Consumer Perspectives, 2007 CDHP Member Experience Report," Blue Cross Blue Shield Association, December 2007.

216 Frank J. Wharam, et al., "Emergency Department Use and Subsequent Hospitalizations Among Members of a High-Deductible Health Plan," *Journal of the American Medical Association,* Vol. 297, No. 10, March 14, 2007.

217 These recommendations are taken from Joseph L. Bast, "Ten Principles of Health Care Policy," *Legislative Principles* No. 3, The Heartland Institute, 2007.

218 Grace-Marie Turner, "Summit Standoff," *Health Policy Matters,* Galen Institute, February 26, 2010.

219 Marc K. Siegel, "Bill Loves American Health Care," *New York Post,* February 25, 2010.

About the Author

Peter Ferrara is director of entitlement and budget policy for the Institute for Policy Innovation and general counsel of the American Civil Rights Union, among other posts. He is the author of "The Obama Health Plan: Rationing, Higher Taxes, and Lower Quality Care" *(Heartland Policy Study* #123, The Heartland Institute, August 2009).

Ferrara has written studies and reports for the Cato Institute, Heritage Foundation, National Center for Policy Analysis, Family Research Council, U.S. Chamber of Commerce, and a wide range of other institutions and publications. He has published articles in *The Wall Street Journal, Barron's, Forbes, American Spectator, National Review, Human Events, Weekly Standard, Policy Review*, and elsewhere. He is the author or coauthor of, or contributor to, the following books:

Newt Gingrich, *Real Change* (2009)
Stop the Raid: Social Security, the Biggest Rip Off in History (2008)
Common Cents, Common Dreams: A Layman's Guide to Social Security Privatization (1999)
A New Deal for Social Security (1998)
Free the Mail: Ending the Postal Monopoly (1990)
Religion and the Constitution: A Reinterpretation (1983)
Social Security: Averting the Crisis (1983)
Social Security: The Inherent Contradiction (1980)

Ferrara served as a senior staff member in the White House Office of Policy Development under President Ronald Reagan and as associate deputy attorney general under President George H.W. Bush. He also has served as an associate professor of law at the George Mason University School of Law. He received an undergraduate degree in economics *magna cum laude* from Harvard College and a J.D. *cum laude* from Harvard Law School. He has practiced law with firms on Wall Street and in Washington, DC.

About The Heartland Institute

The Heartland Institute is a nonprofit, nonpartisan research organization based in Chicago. Founded in 1984, it is devoted to discovering, developing, and promoting free-market solutions to social and economic problems.

The Heartland Institute contacts more elected officials, more often, than any other think tank in the United States. According to a telephone survey of 500 randomly selected state and local officials conducted by Victory Enterprises in 2009, 85 percent of state legislators and 63 percent of local officials say they read and rely on Heartland publications.

Heartland publishes six monthly public policy newspapers – *Budget & Tax News*, *Environment & Climate News*, *FIRE Policy News*, *Health Care News*, *InfoTech & Telecom News*, and *School Reform News* – featuring the best research and commentary from the nation's free-market think tanks and advocacy groups.

Heartland also manages nine Web sites, including its home site at www.heartland.org and a social networking site at www.freedompub.org. It also created and hosts PolicyBot, an online database and search engine for the work of some 350 think tanks and advocacy groups.

Approximately 120 academics and professional economists participate in Heartland's peer review process, and more than 180 elected officials serve on its Legislative Forum. Heartland's full-time staff of government relations professionals interacts daily with hundreds of elected officials across the country, and its public relations and media specialists help shape public opinion by writing and placing dozens of letters to the editor and opinion editorials each week.

Heartland has offices in Chicago, Illinois and Washington, DC, a full-time staff of 35, and a 2010 budget of $7 million. It is supported by the voluntary contributions of approximately 1,800 supporters. For more information, please visit our Web site at www.heartland.org, call 312/377-4000, or write to The Heartland Institute, 19 South LaSalle Street, Suite 903, Chicago, Illinois 60603.